the art of systems thinking

Essential Skills for Creativity and Problem Solving

Joseph O'Connor and Ian McDermott

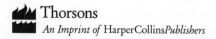

Thorsons
An Imprint of HarperCollins*Publishers*

Thorsons
An Imprint of HarperCollins*Publishers*
77–85 Fulham Palace Road
Hammersmith, London W6 8JB

1160 Battery Street
San Francisco, California 94111–1213

Published by Thorsons 1997

10 9 8 7 6 5 4 3 2

A catalogue record for this book
is available from the British Library

ISBN 0 7225 3442 6

Printed and bound in Great Britain by
Caledonian International Book Manufacturing Ltd, Glasgow

contents

PART FOUR – DRAWING CONCLUSIONS

PART FIVE – CLOSING THE CIRCLE

PART SIX – RESOURCES

To Lara and Frith, and Matthew and Christian, who are the next generation, and who will influence systems we can barely imagine.

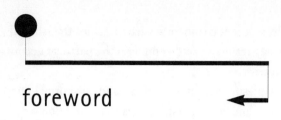

foreword

Throughout the development of this book I thought about how important it was, how it represented such great potential value to all of us. And when I was asked me to write the foreword, I was quite humbled.

Why is this an important book for our time? It is important because of the understanding it can help us develop – understanding why the world we have created has become apparently so complicated, and what to do about it. Over time we have woven the fabric of our existence ever tighter, and with ever more rapid interactions. And, when we do not understand the complexity we have created, we feel helpless, and become victims of what we do not understand.

Why is it that as we approach our goals they seem to be more difficult to achieve? Why is it that things progressing so well seem sooner or later to turn sour? And when things turn sour, how is it that they seem to do so in such a rapid fashion? Why is it that every problem we solve seems simply to lead to a whole new set of problems? Why is it that the problems we thought we solved yesterday seem to come back to haunt us in a few weeks or months? Why is it that a group of individuals each doing what seems so sensible manages to create something that none of them want, i.e. bureaucracy? Why is it that no matter how much money I make it never seems to be enough? Why is it that co-operative partnerships that should produce synergy results so often end with the partners becoming adversaries?

The list of questions is rather endless, and our normal pursuit from a cause and effect perspective is to try and find where the fault lies. A systems thinking perspective, however, enables us to understand the foundations of such situations and why simply fault-finding is such a futile activity. Systems thinking enables one to progress beyond simply seeing events to seeing patterns of interaction and the underlying structures which are responsible for the patterns. And, once we understand the real foundations for the situations we experience, we are in a much better position to respond in an enlightened fashion. We are able to act responsibly and interact with the structures in ways which will enhance or improve the situation without creating new and different problems elsewhere.

Systems thinking is a perspective that we can all relate to, as examples of it can be repeatedly found in our everyday lives. Peter Senge's *The Fifth Discipline* (Doubleday, 1994) has contributed greatly toward popularizing it, yet his context is that of organizational learning, wherein systems thinking was the fifth of five disciplines. My own thought as I read Senge's book, five times in five years, was that it should have been called 'The First Discipline', as the other four disciplines are essentially *applied* systems thinking.

The Art of Systems Thinking enables us to develop an understanding of systems thinking, why it's so important to us in our daily lives, and how one and all can benefit from the understanding. Once we embrace the complexity we have created, and find the simplicity on the other side, we no longer need be victims, for we can use our understanding to change our actions, and thereby our world.

You have probably heard of the butterfly effect, where it was proposed that a butterfly flapping its wings in Miami could cause a hail storm in Beijing. Our actions today have more immediate far-reaching consequences, which was simply not the case in the past. And the pace of our interactions continues to increase. So systems thinking is a perspective more important for our time than any other we have ever had the opportunity to embrace.

I would like to express my sincere appreciation to the authors for investing the thought and effort required to provide this opportunity for understanding to the world.

Gene R. Bellinger
Annandale
Virginia, USA
February 1997

acknowledgements

Many thanks to Gene Bellinger and Gill Norman-Bruce for their great help and encouragement in writing this book.

Our thanks too go to Mike Goodman, Rick Karash and Mark Furman for valuable feedback.

Thank you as well to our editor Carole Tonkinson for her enthusiasm and support.

'Autobiography in Five Short Chapters' by Portia Nelson is from the book *There's a Hole in My Sidewalk* (Beyond Words Publishing Inc., Hillsborough, Oregon, 1993). Our thanks to the publishers for permission to use this story.

We gratefully acknowledge all those who have built the study of systems and systems thinking as a discipline. We have done our best to honour the main contributions in the chapter 'A Brief History of Systems Thinking' in the Resources section.

The systems archetypes described in Part Three were developed at Innovation Associates in the mid-1980s, primarily by Michael Goodman, Jennifer Kemeny and Peter Senge, partly based on work by John Sternman. Some archetypes were foreshadowed by the generic structures which Jay Forrester and other system thinkers had described 20 years earlier.

The causal loop systems diagrams were drafted with Vensim Systems Software. The Personal Learning Edition software is free for academic and personal use and runs on both PC and Macintosh computers.

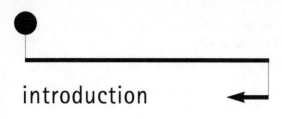

introduction

No man is an island entire of itself; every man is a part of the main. Any man's death diminishes me because I am involved in mankind, and therefore never send to know for whom the bells tolls; it tolls for thee.

John Donne (1572–1631)

This book is about a way of thinking called systems thinking. Systems thinking is seeing beyond what appear to be isolated and independent incidents to deeper patterns. So you recognize connections between events and are therefore better able to understand and influence them.

What is a system? A system is something that maintains its existence and functions as a whole through the interaction of its parts. Your body is the perfect example. It consists of many different parts and organs, each acting separately yet all working together and each affecting the others. The eye cannot see, the legs cannot move without a blood supply. The movement of the legs helps pump the blood back to the heart. The heartbeat – and digestion – are affected by your thoughts; the state of your digestion in turn affects your thoughts – especially after a large lunch. The body is a complex system, and so are a family, a business and a set of beliefs. The environment itself is a very complex system, and one we need to understand much better than we do, as pollution makes many regions unpleasant at best, uninhabitable at worst, and experts argue about the global impact of industrial development.

As our world is becoming increasingly interconnected, so distant events are able to disturb our lives. Tension in the Middle East appears in the local garage as an increase in the price of petrol. Policy changes at governmental level affect our jobs. Intangible rumours can change neighbourhood property prices. We live as a system in a world of systems. To make sense of it we need systems thinking skills.

Experts and politicians who are called to solve problems of pollution and economics often make the situation worse, although with the best of intentions. Ever more information is available, but there is less guidance about what is *useful*. Without this discrimination, more information is simply confusing.

It certainly seems a good idea to look ahead, to plan and anticipate the long-term consequences of our actions, but how exactly can it be done? Even on a personal level, our life, work, finances and relationships may not turn out the way we want or expect, despite our best efforts. What we thought was under our control often seems to develop a mind of its own. Faced with such complexity, it often seems too much to deal with. If only we had a magic mirror that would let us see just a little into the future!

Systems thinking is the way we can discern some rules, some sense of patterns and events, so we can prepare for the future and gain some influence over it. It gives us some measure of control.

A somewhat esoteric, academic air has clung to the subject of systems, as if it were hard to fathom, the province of learned mathematicians and engineers. The very word 'system' may conjure up blackboards filled with squiggly, impenetrable, algebraic formulae. In fact the opposite is true. Systems thinking is practical – and systems are all around us. So you won't need any special mathematical skills to read and understand this book. And you do not have to be able to dismantle a thermostat or solve a differential equation to see the great value of systems thinking and start using it.

What are the benefits of systems thinking?

■ You will be able to gain influence over your life by seeing patterns that drive events. This means you will have more control over your health, your work, your finances and your relationships. You will be able to predict events and prepare for them rather than be helpless in their wake.

■ You will have more effective ways of dealing with problems, better thinking strategies. Not only will you solve problems, but you will also be able to change the thinking that led to the problem in the first place.

■ Your 'trying harder' days will be over, or at least severely curtailed. Problem solving is often like pushing on a 'stuck' door to open it, only to find that the door opens towards you. Systems thinking is finding out which side the hinges are on and in which direction the door opens. Once you know, a small push (or pull) in the right direction is enough.

■ Systems thinking is a basis for clear thought and communication, a way of seeing more and further. Obvious explanations and majority views are not always right. With a wider and different perspective, you can see exactly what is happening and then take actions that you know are best in the long run.

■ Systems thinking will help you to go beyond blaming others or yourself. Most blame is misdirected, for people are usually doing the best they can in the system they are in. It is the

structure of the system, not the effort of the people in it, that
determines the outcome. The way to gain more influence is to
understand the structure of the system.

■ Systems thinking is an essential tool in helping you to manage
yourself and others more effectively. In business, it will help
you understand the complexity of a process so you can see
how to improve it. Systems thinking also helps with teams
and team building, because teams act as a system.

If systems thinking is so wonderful, why is it not better known?
First, because it has tended to be used mostly in technical and
mathematical pursuits, and so confined to academia. It is only
recently that the ideas have become available to a wider
audience. Secondly, education lags behind innovation; the education system is slow to respond to new ideas. School and university curricula are drawn up to last for years and they take
years to complete. So there is always a delay between what is
current in society and what is in the school syllabus. Systems
thinking is just beginning to be taught in some schools. We are
sure this trend will grow.

We are taught to think logically, to understand by analysing –
breaking events into pieces and then reassembling them.
Sometimes this succeeds. But there are problems in applying this
way of thinking indiscriminately. It does not work when dealing
with systems. People and events are not governed by the rules of
logic, they are not as easily predictable and solvable as mathematical equations. So they defy quick, orderly, logical solutions.

The reason habitual thinking is insufficient to deal with systems is because it tends to see simple sequences of cause and effect that are limited in time and space, rather than as a combination of factors that mutually influence each other. In a system, cause and effect may be far apart in time and space. The effect may not be apparent until days, weeks, even years later. And still we have to act now. The long-term effects may be good – good parenting creates caring, resourceful children who in turn become good parents; a wise corporate decision can lead to opening a new, rewarding market months later, when at the time it seemed impossible; an investment on the stock market in one year can lead to a lot of money later. Alternatively, they may be harmful – pesticides and industrial chemicals, for example, have far-reaching effects on the environment that we may discover only after decades of use. We are still unsure of the long-term effects of many of the chemicals we are releasing into the ground, the water supply and the air we breathe. We can only hope that if there are serious effects, it will not be too late to reverse them.

Unless you can connect cause with effect, it is hard to learn from experience and make good decisions. Logical analysis can lead you astray and the obvious solution may make the situation worse, while the eventual remedy may be contrary to common sense. For example, faced with a forest fire, it makes sense to put it out directly. However, if the fire has taken hold, it may not be possible to get enough water to the right place to make a difference. The wind may change and as quickly as you put it out in one place, it spreads in another direction. What do you do? You start fires of your own. You burn selected areas with small controlled fires, then when the main fire reaches them, there is nothing there for it to feed on, so it goes out, defeated by its own hunger. Another example is when you feel anxious before a challenge. Trying to combat anxiety by denying it usually has little effect. Paradoxically, admitting it, feeling it fully and then focusing on something else will stop it.

A complex system may behave in ways that cannot be predicted from looking at the individual parts. For example, when your body systems are working well, you feel good. This sense of well-being is not in your heart, lungs or liver; you will not find it in a particular part of your body. It is something you experience as a *whole system*. And because your body is a system, systems thinking will enable you to look after your physical health and well-being. You will do more of those things that enhance your well-being and less, if any, of those that diminish it.

Systems thinking is not confined to your health. The same structures can be at work in any complex system. So, because the natural world is a system, systems thinking is knowing how to grow flowers and tend a garden, and how to act wisely in the environment. It is about doing the best you can for your partner and your children, because your family is a system. It is about clear thinking, because your beliefs are a system. It applies to managing your finances, because your finances are a system. So are the organizations and businesses you work for and deal with. In fact you already know a lot about systems thinking. You have to. You live in a world of systems. But this book will build on what you know intuitively, and, because your mind and body also form a system, you will come to know yourself better.

HOW TO USE THIS BOOK

This book is arranged in five sections:

- ■ The first is a general introduction to the main ideas of systems thinking with everyday examples.
- ■ The second deals with our belief systems or mental models. Our

beliefs and values form a system. They direct our behaviour and cannot be isolated from the way we perceive and influence external systems. (From here you can explore those sections that interest you, because this book is a system too and all the parts interrelate.)

■ The third section looks at different perspectives and how systems thinking widens our view, so we can be more creative and effective in solving problems.

■ The fourth section deals with so-called 'systems archetypes' – those patterns that recur like familiar storylines in different parts of our lives. You will learn to recognize them and deal with them in your business, health and relationships.

■ The fifth section draws together the threads and suggests some practical applications.

■ The final part is a resources section, providing a glossary, bibliography and a short history of systems thinking.

We hope this book opens many new rewarding paths.

Joseph O'Connor and Ian McDermott
January 1997

Autobiography in Five Short Chapters

CHAPTER ONE

I walk down the street.
There is a deep hole in the
    sidewalk.
I fall in.
I am lost... I am helpless.
It isn't my fault.
It takes forever to find a way out.

CHAPTER TWO

I walk down the same street.
There is a deep hole in the
    sidewalk.
I pretend I do not see it.
I fall in again.
I can't believe I am in this same
    place.
But it isn't my fault.
It still takes a long time to get out.

CHAPTER THREE

I walk down the same street.
There is a deep hole in the
    sidewalk.
I see it is there.
I fall in... it's a habit... but my eyes
    are open.
I know where I am.
It is my fault.
I get out immediately.

CHAPTER FOUR

I walk down the same street.
There is a deep hole in the
    sidewalk.
I walk round it.

CHAPTER FIVE

I walk down a different street.

Portia Nelson

part 1

thinking past
the obvious

1

what is a system?

A million candles can be lit from one flame.

This book is an introduction to systems thinking – what systems are, the key ideas they embody, how to think about them and why they are important. What do we mean by a 'system'? We are going to use the word in its everyday, intuitive sense:

> A system is an entity that maintains its existence and functions as a whole through the interaction of its parts.

Systems thinking looks at the whole, and the parts, and the connections between the parts, studying the whole in order to understand the parts. It is the opposite to reductionism, the idea that something is simply the sum of its parts. A collection of parts that do not connect is not a system. It is a heap.

A System

Interconnecting parts functioning as a whole.	

Changed if you take away pieces or add more pieces. If you cut a system in half, you do not get two smaller systems, but a damaged system that will probably not function.

The arrangement of the pieces is crucial.

The parts are connected and work together.

Its behaviour depends on the total structure. Change the structure and the behaviour changes.

A Heap

A collection of parts.

Essential properties are unchanged whether you add or take away pieces. When you halve a heap, you get two smaller heaps.

The arrangement of the pieces is irrelevant.

The parts are not connected and can function separately.

Its behaviour (if any) depends on its size or on the number of pieces in the heap.

When you look at the patterns that connect the parts rather than simply the parts themselves, a remarkable fact emerges. Systems made from very different parts having completely different functions follow the same general rules of organization. Their behaviour depends on how the parts are connected, rather than what the parts are. Therefore you can make predictions about their behaviour without knowing the parts in detail. You can understand and influence very different systems – your body, your business, your finances and your relationships – using the same principles. Instead of seeing separate fields of knowledge all needing years of study to understand, systems thinking lets you see the connection between different disciplines. It enables you to predict the behaviour of systems, whether the system is a road traffic network, a belief system, a digestive system, a management team or a marketing campaign.

Why is systems thinking so important? Because, as already mentioned, you are a system living in a world of systems. We live in the hugely complex system of the natural environment, and build towns and cities that also work as systems. We have mechanical systems like computers, cars and automated factories. We talk of political systems, economic systems and belief systems. Each one works as a complete functioning whole that combines many separate parts (although how *well* it functions is another matter entirely). Systems can be simple, like a central heating thermostat, or very complex, like the weather. At present we face unprecedented problems due to the impact of pollution and technology on the system we call 'nature'. Wherever we look there are systems. We study molecules, cells, plants and animals as systems. You are made of cells, which in turn build into organ systems, under the control of the nervous system. You are part of your family system, which is turn is part of a local community, which joins other communities to form cities, regions and nations. They are all systems in their own right and subsystems of a larger system. The planet Earth itself can be looked on as a system, part of the solar system, the galaxy and even the universe. We may use the word 'system' lightly, but systems are interwoven into everything we do and in order to gain more influence over them, to gain a better quality of life, we need to understand how they work.

A system, then, is a number of parts acting as a single entity. It may itself be composed of many smaller systems or form part of a larger system. Within the body, for instance, there is the digestive system, the immune system, the nervous system and the blood system. You can study any of these in isolation and also how they work together in the larger system of the human body. A car is a mechanical system made up of different sub-systems: the cooling system, the exhaust system and the fuel system. All these systems work together to produce the smoothly working car that takes you where you want to go. You do not bother to think about the smaller systems until the car breaks down and then you discover why reductionism is so frustrating. You have all the bits of the car, but if they are not working together it is basically a heap of scrap metal.

There is a limit to how big a man-made system can grow. Everything else being equal, at a certain point it will become unwieldy, hard to manage and more prone to breakdown. So, as systems grow bigger, it makes sense to divide them into smaller systems and establish different levels of control. In a business, say, a team of six may work well together, but a team of 600 would not be able to do anything unless it divided itself into smaller groups. There is also a limit to how large anything in the natural world can grow and still live. In the world of systems, bigger does not mean better, it usually means worse. Every system has an optimum size and if it is made much larger or smaller than this without other changes, it will not function.

Emergence – Whirlpools and Rainbows

There are some startling implications to our simple definition of a system. First, systems function as a whole, so they have properties above and beyond the properties of the parts that comprise them. These are known as *emergent properties* – they 'emerge' from the system when it is working. Imagine 100 pictures of Mickey Mouse all slightly different. Not very interesting. Now run them very quickly one after another and Mickey seems to move. You've got a cartoon. When the different pictures are a smooth progression, the movement is also smooth. It is an emergent property.

Because we live with emergent properties, we take them for granted. Yet they are often unpredictable and surprising. (We suppose 'emergency' really ought to be the word here rather than the rather clumsy 'emergent properties', but language has hijacked 'emergency' for unpredictable, sudden and usually unpleasant surprises – a pity.)

Emergent properties arise from systems like those three-dimensional pictures that suddenly pop out from the random swathes of coloured patterns in the infuriating and attractive 'magic eye' books. There is no way you can predict the picture from the pattern you immerse yourself in. Likewise, watch the turbulent flow of water in a river. No amount of knowledge of the molecular structure of water would prepare you for a whirl-pool. (Nor would it let you predict the wetness of water!) You could study acoustics and the physics of sound for years without suspecting the beauty and emotional power of music. Put two eyes together and you do not simply get a bigger picture but three-dimensional vision. Two ears do not simply give you the ability to hear twice as well, they give you the ability to hear in stereo. When you put together the colours of the spectrum, you do not get a muddy brown, but white light. We take these daily miracles for granted, but would you have predicted them if you did not know them already? Properties can emerge like the beauty of a rainbow when the rain, atmosphere and angle of sunlight fit together absolutely right.

Our brains seem to delight in creating these emergent properties. And remember that we are part of the system, for without our senses these properties would not exist.

Consciousness itself is an emergent property. Who could have predicted that the billions of interconnections in the brain would allow the feeling of being aware of ourselves? And all your senses are part of your whole self. You see, not your eyes. Put an eye by itself on the table and it would see nothing. You cannot find sight, hearing, touch, taste or smell in any of the parts of a body. Your life is dependent on your parts working together. When the parts are isolated from the body, they die. Post mortems do not discover the secret of life, but death.

To take another example, the movement of a car is also an emergent property. A car needs a carburettor and the fuel tank in order to move, but put the carburettor or the fuel tank on the road and see how far they go on their own.

The balance of nature, too, is an emergent property. Plants, animals and weather conditions work together to create a flourishing environment, even though within that environment animals may prey on each other. When the environment is disturbed, that particular balance may be lost, some species may die out, others may dominate, but overall, another balance will emerge.

In short:

Systems have emergent properties that are not found in their parts. You cannot predict the properties of a complete system by taking it to pieces and analysing its parts.

When you take a system apart, you do not find its essential properties anywhere. These properties arise only when the whole system is working. The only way to find out what they are is to run the system.

Emergent Properties

Here are some emergent properties. Can you think of more?

- life
- whirlpools
- tornadoes
- temperature
- pressure
- computer software bugs
- computer graphics
- emotions
- music
- magic eye graphics
- rainbows
- culture
- flames
- consciousness
- team morale
- clouds
- health and well-being
- hunger
- laughter
- memories
- dreams
- pain

The nice thing about emergent properties is that you do not have to understand the system to benefit – you do not have to have a degree in electronics to switch on the light, nor understand how a car works to drive. You don't have to understand the millions of lines of software code before playing a computer game. Do you know how computer graphics appear on the screen? Joseph never really thought about it, until one day, as he switched off his computer, his eight-year-old daughter asked him, 'Daddy, where do the pictures go when you switch off?'

'They don't really go anywhere. The computer just doesn't make them any more.'

'But how does the computer remember to make the same picture when you switch on again?'

'They're stored in the computer's memory.'

'What! All those pictures?'

'No, more like how to make them when we tell it to.'

'Where is its memory?'

Joseph started to flounder.

'The computer stores the picture as a pattern of bits that mark the exact position of every small part, so it can remake the whole picture when we ask it to.'

'Where does it store the bits?'

'In the bits of plastic and metal inside the computer we call chips.'

'If we look inside the chips can we see the pictures?'

We had reached the veil between the worlds of silicon and sight.

'No, they're too small.'

'Could we see them with a magnifying glass?'

'No, they are more like patterns of bits like a jigsaw puzzle that the computer knows how to put together. When you tip out the pieces of your jigsaw puzzle, you have to put the pieces together.'

She wasn't very impressed with the explanation, but trying to explain the electrical flows inside a computer with graphics as an emergent property would have been even worse. We cannot break open the computer casing to look for the picture, just as we would not take apart a piano to look for the sound.

'Emergent properties' is also a charitable name for computer bugs. Have you ever had the experience of a computer suddenly behaving very oddly for no apparent reason, while you are doing something you have done hundreds of times before without any problems? We certainly have. Sometimes the computer seems to be actively mischievous or even malevolent. (Shortly after typing this, the computer decided to give us a 'live' demonstration – the program crashed. It wouldn't type, delete or save anything. Cursing the inert heap of silicon, and simultaneously grateful we had saved a few moments before, we rebooted the computer.)

The second critical feature of systems is a mirror image of the first. Just as the properties of the system are shown by the whole system and not by its parts, so if you take the system apart it loses those properties. When you take a piano apart, for example, not only will you not find the sound, but it is also impossible to produce the sound until you reassemble it. You cannot find a rainbow in the rain or a picture inside a television. When you cut a system in half, you do not get two smaller systems, but a broken or dead system.

Analysis is the name for taking something to pieces to find out how it works. This is very useful for certain types of problems or for seeing how a large system is made up of smaller subsystems. *You gain knowledge through analysis.* However, you cannot understand the whole system properties by breaking the system into its constituent parts.

The complement of analysis is synthesis – building the parts into a whole. *You gain understanding through synthesis.* The only way to find out how a system functions and what its emergent properties are is to see it in action as a whole.

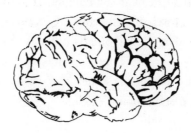

The Most Complex System We Think We Know

The world is a very complex system. We need a complex system to make sense of it.

The human brain is the most complex structure within the known universe. Weighing 3–4 lb (around 1.5 kg), it consists of over 100 billion neurons or nerve cells – as many stars as there are in the Milky Way. The front part of the brain, or cerebral cortex, has over 10 billion neurons. The connections *between* the nerve cells are more important than the cells themselves, just as systems thinking would suggest. A single neuron can have up to 100,000 inputs and continually integrate 1,000 inputs. The brain is not like a computer, but every nerve cell works like a small computer. The cortex has over one million billion connections. If you were to count one every second, it would take you 32 million years.

No two brains are alike. We are born with all the neurons we need, but up to 70 per cent of them will die in our first year of life. The surviving neurons form an ever more complex web of connections. Certain connections are reinforced by use and others wither as we learn about the world. The brain is not independent of the world, it is shaped by it – the outside system of the world moulds the inside system of our brain.

The brain has the task of extracting pattern and sense from the huge flood of sensory information it receives. The very act of perception also makes meaning of that perception and so the brain in turn shapes the world as it appears to us. Interpretation is part of sensation.

The brain has been described by neuroscientists as an interconnected, decentralized, parallel processed, distributed network of simultaneous waves of interactive resonance patterns. In other words, a very complex system.

The brain is every bit as complex as our vanity hoped and our intellect feared.

Simple and Complex Systems

A system maintains itself through the interaction of its parts, and so it is the relationships and the mutual influence between the parts that is important, rather than the number or size of the parts. These relationships, and therefore the systems, can be simple or complex.

There are two very different ways that anything can be complicated. When we think something is complex, we usually think of it having many different parts. That is complexity of detail. When you look at a 1,000-piece jigsaw puzzle, you are looking at complexity of detail. We can usually find a way of simplifying, grouping and organizing this sort of detail, and there is only one place for every piece to fit. Computers are good at dealing with this sort of complexity, especially if it can be sequenced.

The other type of complexity is dynamic complexity. This is when the elements can relate to each other in many different ways, because each part has many different possible states, so a few parts can be combined in a myriad of different ways. It is misleading to judge complexity on the number of separate bits, rather than the possible ways of putting them together. It is not necessarily true that the smaller the number of parts, the simpler to understand and deal with. It all depends on the degree of dynamic complexity.

Consider a business project team. Each person's mood can change from moment to moment. There are many, many different ways they can relate to each other. So a system may have a few parts but a great deal of dynamic complexity. Problems that look simple on the surface may reveal a great deal of dynamic complexity when we probe them.

New connections between parts of a system add complexity and adding another piece can create many new connections. When you add one new piece, the number of *possible connections* does not increase by one. It may increase *exponentially* – in other words, for every one you add you get a bigger increase than you got from adding the one before it. For example, suppose you start with just two pieces, A and B. There are two possible links and pathways of influence: A on B and B on A. Now let's add another part. Now there are three parts: A, B and C. The number of possible connections, however, has increased to six; 12 if we allow two parts to form alliances and influence the third (e.g. A plus B influences C). You can see that it does not take many parts to create a dynamically complex system, even when the parts have only one state. We know this from experience – two people are more than twice as hard to manage as one, there is more chance of difficulty miscommunication, and a second child brings far more than twice the work and twice the joy to the parents.

The simplest systems will have a few parts that have only a few states and a few simple relationships between those parts. A plumbing system or a thermostat are good examples. They have limited detail complexity and limited dynamic complexity.

A very complex system may have many parts or subsystems, all of which can have different states which may change in response to other parts. Mapping this kind of complex system would be like finding your way through a maze that changed itself completely depending on what direction you took at any time. A game involving strategy, like chess, is a game of dynamic complexity because whenever you make a move you alter the whole board because your move changes the relationships between the pieces. (An even more dynamically complex chess game would have a piece changing into a different piece every time it made a move!)

The first lesson of systems thinking is to know whether you are dealing with detail or dynamic complexity – a jigsaw or a chess game.

The relationship between the different parts of the system determines how it works, so each part, however small, can affect the behaviour of the whole. For example, your hypothalamus, a small gland the size of a pea which is located in the middle of your brain, regulates your temperature, breathing rate, water balance and blood pressure. Likewise your heart rate affects your whole body. When it speeds up you may feel anxious, excited or exhilarated. When it slows down you feel more relaxed.

All parts of a system are interdependent, they all interact. How they relate to each other gives them the power to affect the whole system. This suggests an interesting rule for influencing systems, particularly groups: the more connections you have, the more possible influence. Networking brings influence. Indeed, research suggests that successful managers spend four times as much time networking as their less successful colleagues.[1]

Different parts can also combine to affect the whole. Groups form alliances that make a difference in government, organizations and teams.

The System as a Web

Complex systems are bound together by many links, so they are usually very stable. The French phrase *plus ça change, plus c'est la même chose* sums it up perfectly: whatever changes also stays the same in important ways. It is easy to see why this is so. Imagine a system as a kind of web with each part influencing and connected to many others. The more parts there are, the more complex the system is in detail. The more the parts can change state and form shifting alliances, the more possible con- nections there are between the parts, and the more dynamically complex the system.

Imagine a complex system like a web. Say, some of the possible elements of the government of a fictional state called Dystopia *(see figure)*. You could also make this hypothetical system represent a business, where the factors are such things as established procedures, job responsibilities, reward and appraisal systems and management styles. It could also be made to represent people in an organization, factors in an advertising campaign, different ideas in a belief system, a team, an extended family or parts of your body.

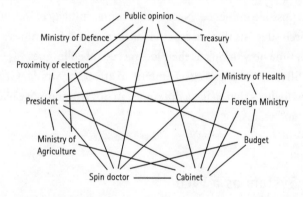

The government of Dystopia

This system has 11 elements. Let's suppose the government is stable, all the pieces fit together and the system works. The links between the parts keep it steady. Now, imagine you want to change how the budget is calculated, but you cannot do this without taking all the other pieces it is linked to into account.

Changing it will affect all the other parts of the system that it is linked to. They will resist the change because it means they will have to change as well.

This is the problem with political reforms. The political system is very complex and many a political career has ended in disappointment because the system resists change. New governments inherit a vast bureaucracy that is notoriously cautious. The BBC television comedy *Yes, Minister* showed the hapless government minister Jim Hacker (later promoted beyond his level of competence to Prime Minister) struggling in vain against the Machiavellian wiles of his civil servants. Whatever initiative he wanted to take, whatever shift he wanted to make, somehow he always seemed to end up reinforcing the very system he wanted to change. The Civil Service was the personification of the resistance of a complex system to the quick change (or indeed any change).

A system will act like a strong elastic net – when you pull one piece out of position it will stay there only for as long as you actually exert force on it. When you let go, you may be surprised and annoyed that it springs back to where it was before. Yet when you see this obstinacy as part of a system rather than isolated maliciousness, its resistance is not only understandable but inevitable.

New Year's resolutions are a good example. Suppose you have a habit you want to change. A habit, especially if you do not approve of it, seems to be 'outside' you, something you could just drop and be the better for it. But these habits are part of your total system of behaviour. You may not like them, but they connect with many other parts of your life. On New Year's Day you resolve to change, but somehow the habit persists unless you make a constant effort. You feel the strain – literally. Trying harder may not help. It is not the habit or behaviour that is so strong in itself – the strength of resistance comes from all the other parts that it is bound into. You are not just pulling on it alone, but on all the habits and experiences it links to. From a systems thinking point of view, you would expect such resolutions to be very difficult to keep.

Stability and Leverage

How stable a system is depends on many factors, including the size, number and variety of the subsystems within it and the type and degree of connectivity between them. A complex system is not necessarily an unstable one. Many complex systems are remarkably stable and therefore resistant to change. For example, different political parties can gain power without the whole democratic system of government being overthrown. Families tolerate arguments and disagreements without falling apart, and businesses can still function even when there are policy disagreements between different departments. Also, part of your body may not work very well, yet overall you can still function. This stability is really important, for without it your health would fluctuate wildly, businesses would fail or boom erratically and every disagreement would threaten your friendships. This overall stability is a positive aspect, but it comes (of course) with a price. The price is resistance to change.

So political parties struggle with their civil servants and reforms meet a constant series of checks. Families may be unhappy, but they live with it. New business practices are usually resisted, as people feel comfortable with the old ways of doing things. It is not that people are being difficult, it is the system that they are in. Whenever you make a change in any complex system – a business, a family or your own way of doing things – expect resistance. You cannot have stability without resistance, they are two sides of the same coin.

Reformers often make the mistake, particularly in business, of pushing and pushing, and finally exhausting the system's resilience, at which point it breaks down completely, to everybody's cost.

When systems do change, they tend to do so relatively rapidly and often quite drastically. The Berlin Wall is a good example. It had divided East and West Berlin since August 1961, a symbol of the East German government's long-standing hostility towards the West, yet in November 1989 the government collapsed and the wall was demolished by enthusiastic people using their bare hands in an incredible scene of elation and release. There were many political and economic reasons behind this, it was not a simple process, but the actual event was quick and dramatic. At the same time, Communist governments that had been stable for decades were falling one after another.

When pressure for change builds up in a system, it can suddenly burst like a balloon. There is a threshold beyond which a system will suddenly change or break down. If the system is under a lot of pressure it only takes a small trigger, just as a small crack in a dam can lead to its collapse because of the pressure of water behind it. The more stressed you feel, the less provocation it takes for you to lose your temper. It is the straw that breaks the camel's back.

So, if you put a system under enough pressure for long enough, it can suddenly collapse. Systems can also suddenly change if you find just the right combination of actions. This comes from understanding the system and is known as *the principle of leverage*. This principle is simple. Again, imagine a system as a web with many parts connected. Suppose you want to change the position of one part. When you pull on it directly, it seems to resist, but really the whole system resists. However, cutting a small link in another place may free this piece, like undoing a crucial knot in a tangle of string. You need to know how the system is made up to know which knot to undo. Ian was working in a business some years ago where it was well known that if you wanted something done in a certain department you had to speak to the secretary of the departmental head. Speaking directly to the senior managers had no effect.

Leverage and sudden change also relate to how smoothly the system functions over time and how it responds in special circumstances. Complex systems are not always smoothly continuous in their behaviour. System behaviour is described as continuous when it behaves predictably through its range of states. For example, you can test a car through its range of speeds and you can be fairly sure that if it works at 70 miles an hour and 10 miles an hour, it will also work at all the speeds in between. It is not suddenly going to come apart at $35\frac{1}{2}$ mile per hour. Its behaviour is continuous throughout the range of speeds.

Living systems and some mechanical systems like computer software may behave very differently. Discontinuous system behaviour is when something weird happens given the right special set of circumstances. The computer crashes, the person loses their temper or the body becomes ill. The possibility was always there, it's just that the exact circumstances never cropped up in the tests, that the system is too complex to control all the variables. Two pieces of software that work perfectly well on their own may not work together and cause the computer to crash. Two people who do excellent work independently may be at each other's throats when they work together.

Medical drugs are another example. They have to undergo stringent tests over a long period. But even so, many drugs react badly with other drugs or have side-effects that do not manifest until years afterwards. The presence of another drug, or a long time period (or both), is a special set of circumstances. The more complex the system, the less you can rely on sampling to predict the effects.

The same process is at work when you lose your temper. For example, perhaps you have had a day when everything goes wrong and your mood inexorably worsens. You feel under pressure. Then something trivial happens – another motorist makes a mistake or someone makes a chance remark that irks you. It is the last straw and you explode with anger.

However, there is good news too (of course). If system failure can happen under what seems like trivial circumstances, then other, more desirable changes can also happen with little effort. Change can be surprisingly easy if you identify the right connections. This doesn't mean piling on the pressure, but knowing *where* to intervene so that a small effort can get a huge result. This is *leverage*.

How do you apply the idea of leverage? Instead of wasting effort in directly pulling or pushing, which could exhaust both you and the system, ask the key systems question: *What stops the change?*

Look at the connections that are holding the part you want to change in place. Cut or weaken these and the change may be easy. This is a key principle of systems thinking.

Some parts of a system are more critical than others, that is, they exercise a higher degree of control. A head injury is far more dangerous than a leg injury, because the brain has a higher level of control over the body than the leg. In business, when you make a change at head office, the effects ramify down through all the local branches. Changing a manager at a local branch is less likely to affect the policy of the whole business – although it is possible, as complex systems are full of surprises. As a general rule, however, the greater the control of the system of the part you change, the more pervasive and wide-ranging the effects.

Side-Effects

This leads on to another consequence of the connectedness of the pieces in a system. When you change one part, the influence radiates out like ripples from a stone thrown into a pool. What you do may affect other parts of the system which may then affect still others that are far from the original change.

When you are dealing with a system you can never just do one thing.

Medical drugs are again a good example. All drugs have side-effects. The only question is whether they are noticeable, and if so, how uncomfortable or dangerous the side-effects are and whether they are worth putting up with for the positive effects of the drug. Antibiotics, for instance, are very effective against bacterial infections. The stomach upsets they cause (because they kill the naturally occurring and beneficial bacteria in the gut as well as the dangerous bacteria that have made you ill) are usually a small price to pay.

The side-effects of drugs may appear years after treatment and it is hard to make the connection between the two. For example, steroid drugs are used to treat a whole variety of conditions: inflammation, asthma, eczema and arthritis. Yet they can also cause muscle wasting, high blood sugar, diabetes, water retention, insomnia, mood changes, menstrual problems and osteoporosis, All these are listed in the official *Physician's Desk Reference*. The more powerful the drug, the more likely there are to be side-effects.

Sometimes, however, the side-effects can be utilized in another context. For example, aspirin, as well as being a potent pain reliever, also has the side-effect of thinning the blood when taken in larger quantities. It is a cheap, readily available and familiar drug and is now widely used as a way of preventing strokes in patients who have suffered heart attacks or those with constricted blood vessels. Aspirin still has unpleasant side-effects – stomach upsets, nausea and sometimes allergic responses and anaemia – because it can deplete the body of essential vitamins and minerals, particularly iron.

We are very careful with medical drugs, but not so careful with the equivalents of drugs in our environment – the pesticides and chemicals we use. The most infamous example of this is the insecticide DDT. Invented in 1939 (it helped earn the discoverer a Nobel Prize), it was used by farmers as an insecticide and was particularly effective in controlling mosquitoes and thus preventing the spread of malaria. However, by 1950, there was mounting evidence that DDT was toxic to many animals. By 1970, when its use was finally controlled, it had worked its way up the food chain and was found in human tissue.

Nor was it effective as an insecticide in the long term. At the beginning, the insects ate the DDT but the insectivores (animals who feed on insects) ate the poisoned insects. When

what is a system?

the insectivores started to die, the insect population (which had started to become immune to DDT anyway) increased, so paradoxically, the insect population got larger, not smaller.

Consider, there are over 65,000 industrial chemicals now in regular commercial use and up to five more come on the market every day. Eighty per cent of these chemicals are not tested for toxicity.[2] We are discovering their side-effects to our cost as time passes.

Another principle of systems thinking, then, is:

Expect side-effects.

They may be surprising. They may be unpleasant. But when you do understand the system you can begin to predict them, so that you can design your change to have the desired effects with few detrimental side-effects. Or even you can have the desired change as a side-effect of another change by applying the principle of leverage.

For example, we know a family where one of the children, a boy of 10 named Tom, had got into trouble at his school. He would pick fights with other children in the playground and get into kicking matches with them. He was also extremely demanding in class, continually asking for the teacher's attention. The school spoke with the parents and they all agreed that the family should receive some counselling. After a number of sessions, it turned out that the leverage point was in the parents' attitude to discipline. They set broad limits, because they wanted to encourage the boy to be self-reliant and to discover ideas for himself. They believed that limits are much stronger and better when they are internalized rather than imposed. This approach had worked very well with Tom's older brother. What Tom needed, however, was much clearer boundaries. He needed to be told exactly what to do. Without a clear sense of acceptable boundaries he felt insecure, so he kept pushing to the limit to find out where they were.

As an experiment, and with the counsellor's support, the parents became very directive with Tom. After a few difficult weeks, he started to respond – he became much calmer, stopped fighting at school and started to work in a more self-directed way in class. Paradoxically (again that word!), the parents got the result they wanted by doing the opposite. The effects spread beyond Tom to the parents, to the elder brother and to the school. The class teacher was less stressed and so the whole class was happier.

In this example, no one was to blame and no one wanted the initial situation. Everyone agreed it had to change, but how? The action taken was indirectly on Tom and directly on the parent's beliefs. They acted differently, which led to Tom acting differently.

We shall see that very often the most critical point for leverage in any system is the beliefs of the people in it, because it is the beliefs that sustain the system as it is.

---

1 Luthans, Paul, *Real Managers*, Ballinger Publishing Company, 1988

2 World Commission on Environment and Development, *Our Common Future*, Oxford University Press, 1987

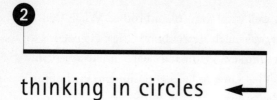
thinking in circles

Feedback Loops – The Essence of Systems

Systems thinking is thinking in loops rather than in straight lines. The parts of a system are all connected directly or indirectly, therefore a change in one part ripples out to affect all the other parts. So, these other parts will change and the effect of this will ripple out in turn to affect the original part. The original then responds to that new influence. Therefore the influence comes back to the original part in a modified way, making a loop, not a one-way street. This is called a *feedback loop*. When two parts are connected, influence can go both ways, like a telephone line – if you can dial a friend, they can equally well dial you. Feedback is the output of a system re-entering as its input, or the return of information to influence the next step.

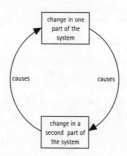

Feedback loop

Our experience is made up of feedback loops, although we usually think of influence in one direction. Try this experiment. Take the tip of your index finger and slowly put it over the full stop at the end of this sentence. You have just demonstrated a feedback loop. Sceptical? Try it again, this time with your eyes closed. You will miss. To hit the target, your eyes must constantly feed you information about the position of your finger *vis-à-vis* the full stop. You make small continuous adjustments in fractions of a second all the way down to the page. You would see this with high speed photography. Closing your eyes proves that you do not aim your finger like an arrow from a bow, once and for all, and then let it go off towards the target. Your eyes constantly measure the difference, if any, between the target and your finger and your muscles act to reduce that difference. You can try the same experiment if you swing a bat or club at a ball – try closing your eyes before you start the swing. Even though the swing goes through very fast, watching the ball does make a difference. Sports coaches never tire of repeating, 'Keep your eye on the ball!' The only way we can receive feedback to direct our actions is through our senses, by seeing, feeling, tasting, smelling and hearing.

We experience feedback as the consequences of our actions coming back to us and so influencing what we do next. 'Feedback' is often used to mean any response, but the essential point is that it is a return of the effects of an action, influencing the next step, i.e. a two-way link. Feedback is a loop, so thinking in terms of feedback is *thinking in circles*.

Criticism is often euphemistically referred to as 'feedback', but it only merits the label if it leads to change in the person criticized. An annual performance review is only feedback when it leads to a change in the person's work, either motivating them to better results or depressing them so they care even less about what they do.

Thirst is a good example of feedback. Think of what happens when you realize you are thirsty – you have an uncomfortable sensation, so you reach for a glass of water. As you drink the water, you feel less thirsty, so you drink less. You keep drinking until you are satisfied, then you stop. Your thirst influenced the amount of water you drank and the water you drank influenced your thirst. We think of it as one action, but when you look at it more closely, it's a loop. It would only be one action if you knew exactly how much water to drink in order to quench our thirst, in advance, and then drank it. Hunger works the same way. You eat until your appetite is satisfied. The feelings of hunger and thirst are part of feedback loops within one system – you.

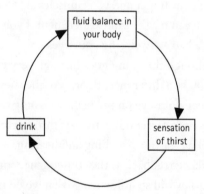

The thirst feedback loop

Now think of a conversation with another person and imagine slowing it right down to see what is happening moment by moment. You think of what to say and say it. Your partner hears the words, which stimulate their own thoughts, and they reply. You respond to their reply. Your output is through your mouth and your body language, your input is the other person's speech and body language, and you get it through your eyes and ears.

Your output becomes their input, which influences their output, which becomes your input ... so the conversation flows. You know what to say next by listening to your partner. Anyone who just talks at other people, ignores their response and is only interested in the sound of their own voice is a bore, and soon finds no one willing to listen.

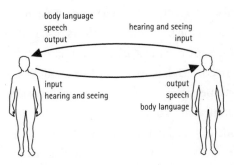

Communication feedback loop

Feedback is so essential to the way we live that when we do not get any directly, we create it. So if you say you will telephone me and do not, I may take that as feedback and believe that you do not care, that you do not think I am important. We cannot *not* communicate because we take even the absence of communication as feedback because feedback is so much part of our experience.

One more example, this time the system of you plus bicycle. First, you have to pedal. If you sit still you will just fall over. As you are moving, your eyes and sense of balance give you feedback, and you have to continually shift your weight to keep your balance and forward movement. A good cyclist will travel in a straight line, but a learner will wobble, because they do not respond so quickly to the feedback and then may overreact. The better you get, the less you wobble, because the quicker you respond and the better you judge how to react. Your eyes and sense of balance supply the input; your output is through the arm and leg muscles. This output (your muscles' movements) changes the state of the system (learner plus bicycle) and so gives new input (stability and direction).

The principle of feedback seems so simple, so ubiquitous, that we live and breathe feedback loops and take them for granted. It hard to appreciate just how important they are.

We can also see feedback loops at work in the machines we build. Feedback is the principle that allows machines to work without direct human control. Machines built with feedback circuits are more powerful, more controllable and do not need constant human supervision. The steam engine, for example, revolutionized existing technology, gave impetus to the industrial revolution and changed our lives and way of working. Now electronic feedback circuits power the information revolution; they form the driving force of computers and all devices that rely on microchip technology, from washing machines to missiles.

To see a simple mechanical feedback device used every day, you need look no further than your bathroom. The float valve keeps the water in the tank of the flush toilet at a constant level. The principle is simple. A large hollow ball floats on top of the water, connected by a series of levers to a valve that opens to allow water in. Flushing the toilet opens another valve that drains the water from the tank, the water level drops and so the float drops too. When the float drops, it lifts the first valve allowing water into the tank. As the tank fills, the water level rises and the float rises with it. The more the float rises, the more it cuts the inflow of water, until, when it is back at the top level where it started, the inflow valve is completely closed again. A very similar system operates in your car controlling the flow of petrol into the engine through the carburettor. Your foot on the accelerator controls the valve or it can be done automatically by the cruise control mechanism – a rather more sophisticated feedback device.

The house thermostat is another classic feedback device. You set the temperature you want. This is the 'goal' of the system. If the house temperature falls below this, as sensed by the thermometer, then it makes a connection that turns on the boiler. The boiler produces heat and raises the temperature. As soon as the thermometer rises again in response, the connection is broken and the boiler shuts down. You set the level and the system does the rest. This system does not cope with hot weather that takes the temperature above your required level – to do that you would have to set another thermostat that turned on the air conditioning when the house got too warm.

Have you noticed that when you open a refrigerator, the motor usually starts up? That is because the open door lets in warmer air. The interior warms slightly and as the thermostat inside the refrigerator is set to a keep a low temperature, it activates the motor to cool it down.

We have our own much more sophisticated thermostat keeping our internal body temperature constant. The body sets the temperature for 98.6° Fahrenheit and you cannot alter *that* setting! When we get hotter several things happen. We begin to perspire and so lose heat through evaporation from the skin. Also, the blood vessels close to our skin dilate so that more blood reaches the surface and heat is lost to the outside. Both these responses are outside our conscious control, they are automatic feedback loops within the body. Our bodies can only tolerate a very small variation on either side of our internal temperature.

Reinforcing Feedback

Feedback is fundamental in systems – no feedback, no system.

There are two basic types of feedback loop:

- The first is *reinforcing feedback* – when the changes in the whole system feed back to amplify the original change. In other words, change goes through the system producing more change in the same direction.
- The second is *balancing feedback* – when the changes in the whole system feed back to oppose the original change and so dampen the effect.

All systems, however complex, consist of just these two types of feedback loop.

First we will look at reinforcing feedback. This is often misleadingly called 'positive' feedback, but this is a misnomer, first because it may become confused with praise, and secondly, because it gives the impression that it is good. It may be good or it may be a disaster, causing the system to spiral out of control; it depends what is being amplified. We will always refer to this type of feedback as 'reinforcing' to avoid confusion.

Reinforcing feedback drives a system in the way it is going. It may lead to growth or decline, depending on the starting conditions. Reward is part of a reinforcing feedback loop if it leads to more of the same behaviour. Reward may be a gift, money, encouragement, attention or even a smile. Your action, the reward and your repeated action is the reinforcing feedback loop. Reward by itself is not reinforcing feedback, unless it leads to more of the same.

Think of a snowball rolling down a hill. It collects snow as it rolls and the larger it becomes, the more snow it collects, until it eventually becomes an avalanche.

Did you know your bank account is a system? A savings account shows reinforcing feedback. Imagine you have £1,000 in a savings account earning 10 per cent interest per annum. In the first year the capital collects £100 interest, making a total of £1,100. In the second year, this new sum collects 10 per cent – £110 – which is added to the capital, making £1,210. The next year it collects still more interest. The larger the sum, the more interest it collects and the interest in turn makes the sum larger. Taking this example further, in just over seven years you would double your money to £2,000. Every seven years it would double again. £1,000 deposited for you at birth would be worth £8,000 on your twenty-first birthday. Unchecked reinforcing feedback leads to exponential growth – the increase is proportional to what is already there – with a constant doubling time. It starts slowly but the bigger it gets, the faster it grows.

To show reinforcing feedback we will use the image of a snowball:

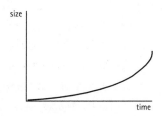

Reinforcing feedback – exponential growth

Exponential Growth – A Quiz

❶ Imagine folding a piece of paper in half so it was twice the thickness. How thick do you think it would be if you were able to fold it another 40 times?

❷ You are the owner of a pond. A small water-lily starts to grow in one corner. You notice it doubles in size every day. It starts very small, but after 30 days you notice it covers half the pond. You do not want it to cover the whole pond, because it would overwhelm all the other flowers, but you are busy and decide to leave it until the last possible day. When will that be?

❸ There is a legend that the game of chess was invented thousands of years ago in the Middle East as a pastime for a king. The inventor asked for a reward from the king: one grain of rice for the first square of the chessboard, two for the second and four for the third, continuing to double the last number for each subsequent square. The chess board has 64 squares. The king knew he had hundreds of huge buildings storing the rice harvest of the kingdom, so he agreed. Was this wise?

Answers on page 58.

Population and Exponential Growth

Population grows exponentially, everything else being equal. In the middle of the seventeenth century the world population was about half a billion people. It was growing, and if the growth rate stayed constant, would double in 150 years.

Two hundred and fifty years later, at the beginning of the twentieth century, the population was over one and a half billion people with a doubling time now of 140 years. The rate of growth was increasing because death rates were falling. In 1991 the world population was nearly five and half billion, birth rates had fallen slightly faster than death rates in the previous 20 years and the population growth rate was about 1.7 per cent. Even such a small growth rate still adds a huge number of people because the population base is so large (it adds 92 million people every year – 2.4 million people every day).

As long as fertility is higher than mortality, that is, birth rate is higher than death rate, the population will grow exponentially. When fertility is the same as mortality, the number will stay steady, an equal number of people being born each year to replace those who die. When mortality is greater than fertility, the population will decline. This is so for every population.

Birth and death rates are not constant throughout the world – in some countries population is increasing, in some it is declining and in others it is steady. The world population growth is the result of all the figures taken together. The latest reports show that the most probable scenario is that the world's population will peak at around 10 and a half billion people in 2080 and then begin to decline.[1]

This is assuming present trends continue – the birth rate all over the world is falling and life expectancy in the Third World is increasing only at a rate of one year per decade.

To recap, reinforcing feedback leads to change in the same direction as the initial change. When the initial change is in a favourable direction, this is a great benefit. But suppose the initial change is unfavourable? Reinforcing feedback can lead to vicious circles as well as virtuous ones.

Take the example of the savings account, or any investment of capital. When there is a positive investment, the reinforcing loop creates more wealth, so more can be invested. If you have no investment, there is no change. But if you owe money, then the debt grows very rapidly. A credit card debt of £1,000 at an annual percentage rate of 20 per cent, for example, grows to £1,200 at the end of one year and £1,440 at the end of two years. Your debt will double in under four years and double again in another four years. Exponential growth means a constant doubling time – whatever the amount.

Reinforcing Feedback Metaphors

Have you used or heard any of these sayings? They usually mean there is a reinforcing loop at work:

- We're on a roll.
- Jump on the bandwagon.
- Downhill all the way.
- Spiralling into oblivion.
- The sky's the limit.
- A ticket to heaven.
- Can do no wrong.
- On the way up.
- On the slippery slope.
- It just keeps getting better (worse) all by itself.
- Snowballing out of control.

But remember, nothing lasts forever!

Reinforcing feedback does not always lead to explosive exponential growth, but it always *amplifies* a change in the same direction. Take communication – this sometimes gets into reinforcing feedback loops. When you start out on friendly terms, it is the equivalent of having money in your account. Good feelings will dominate and both of you will enjoy the encounter. Mutual trust leads to more trust. A neutral encounter is like an empty bank account, it tends to stay neutral, but if you start out on the wrong foot, the situation can go rapidly downhill. Mutual suspicion can work as a reinforcing feedback loop. Also, when people are suspicious of each other, they are likely to misinterpret what the other says and does. They may then feel justified in retaliating in the same vein. If the feedback loop goes unchecked, it can leads to escalating violence and mutual hostility between people or even wars between nations.

Another example of reinforcing feedback making a virtuous circle is the growth of knowledge and learning. Knowledge is intangible, but it is still driven by a reinforcing feedback loop. The more we know, the more we can know, through making connections with what we know already. We can broaden as well as deepen our knowledge.

Now for a vicious circle. An overworked manager does not bring their full concentration to a project. This leads to problems and the work needs to be done again, which adds to the workload...

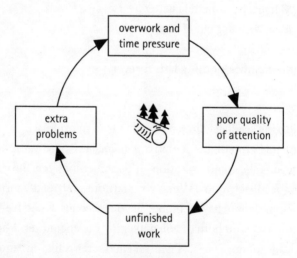

Time pressure as a reinforcing feedback loop

Examples of Reinforcing Feedback

Here are some examples of reinforcing feedback. You will be able to think of many others...

- team morale
- cancer
- paranoia
- amplifier feedback noise
- growth of living cells
- population growth
- savings account interest
- bank debts
- learning
- knowledge
- power
- rumours
- chain letters
- self-confidence
- epidemics of disease
- nuclear reactions
- panic attacks
- coral reefs
- rewards

Balancing Feedback

Nothing grows forever. Eventually the second type of feedback comes in and limits growth. This is called *balancing feedback*. It opposes the change. A balancing feedback loop is where change in one part of the system results in changes in the rest of the system that restrict, limit or oppose the initial change. These are the loops that resist change and keep the system stable, otherwise reinforcing feedback would break it up.

Balancing feedback is sometimes called 'negative' feedback, but this is confusing for two reasons. First, 'negative feedback' is widely understood to mean criticism, and secondly, 'negative' implies it is a bad thing. Balancing feedback on its own is neither good nor bad, it just means the system resists change. This may help or hinder us – it depends what we want to do. If you want to change a complex system, balancing feedback appears as 'resistance'. When you want to maintain the system, it appears as stability.

We have uncounted balancing feedback loops in our body. For example, we maintain a constant body temperature. A small part of the brain called the hypothalamus acts as our body's 'thermostat'. When it detects a difference between our actual temperature and what it ought to be, it triggers the changes that will reduce that difference. Other balancing loops maintain our heartbeat, blood pressure and body temperature in the face of outside changes. We would die if these were not dependable.

A balancing feedback loop is set up by a difference between what the system has – the present conditions – and what the system needs to balance. We will show balancing feedback loops in this book with a picture of a balance:

Most of the examples on pages 26–31 are balancing feedback loops. Thirst is a signal that a difference has opened between the fluid the body needs and the fluid it has. You drink to reduce that difference and balance the system again. When you ride a bicycle, if your eyes and muscles detect too great a difference between where you are and where you want to be, you move your arms and legs to reduce that difference.

Balancing feedback seeks a goal. All systems have balancing feedback loops to stay stable, so all systems have a goal – even if it is only to remain as they are.

Balancing feedback drives the system towards its goal – where the loop will no longer operate and the system will come to rest or be in a balanced state.

Balancing feedback always acts to reduce the difference between where a system is and where it 'should' be. As long as there is a difference between the present state of the system and its desired state, balancing feedback will move the system in the direction of the desired state. The closer the system is to the goal, the smaller the difference represented by the feedback, and so the less the system moves.

A system therefore needs a way of measuring, otherwise it could not tell the difference between where it is and where it should be. The system needs to measure accurately; if it does not, then it risks triggering feedback loops when none are needed. For example, if the thermometer on the thermostat is a few degrees out, it will turn on the boiler at the wrong temperature. Joseph has a series of warning lights on his car dashboard. A few months ago, the brake warning light stayed on and the handbook said this meant the brakes needed immediate attention. When

Joseph took the car to a garage, they found the brakes were fine, but the electronic measuring device had broken, triggering the signal that the brakes were faulty when they were not.

Secondly, the measuring system needs to measure at the right level of detail for the system to work. So, for example, if the thermometer in the thermostat measured in one hundredths of a degree, it might keep putting the boiler on and off every few minutes as the temperature changes microscopically every time someone enters or leaves a room. If, on the other hand, the thermometer measured in increments of five degrees, you might get quite chilly before it turned the heating on. Every system needs to measure with the right degree of precision. In communication, we all know people whose social awareness is so crass that they will ignore your yawn and glazed expression and continue to show you their extensive folder of holiday photographs. On the other hand, there are people who are so oversensitive that they interpret chance remarks as rebukes or a few moments' inattention as a hurtful slight.

To communicate sensibly implies a goal, even if we are not aware of it, otherwise our actions would be simply random. We always act with purpose, however trivial, from the micro level of pointing our finger to the macro level of planning our life. We may be unaware of our goals, change them or fail to achieve them, but they are always there. Every conversation has a purpose, even if only to pass the time of day in a pleasant way. You choose your responses with that in mind. Often we have a very definite purpose – to sell the other person something, to convince them of our point of view or to get them to do what we want. We pick our words and actions depending on our purpose, and feedback from the other person tells us whether we are on track. So if your purpose were to make a sale, for instance, you would follow up your customer's expressions of interest, answer their questions and try to maintain rapport with them.

Since this book is a communication, it was written in a web of balancing feedback loops. First, there was internal balancing feedback changing the book in the process of writing. It was revised and redrafted several times to make it clearer, so that each passage fitted better into the total sense and style. These sentences you are reading now are not the ones originally written. Then there was external balancing feedback from others who read and commented on the manuscript. Friends and colleagues read the drafts, commented, praised and suggested ideas and improvements which were then incorporated into the next draft.

Keeping track of a business inventory involves a balancing feedback loop. There need to be enough goods in stock to satisfy demand, so customers do not have to wait, but not so many that they take up space needed for some other commodity, so the business has to pay high storage charges. Supply and demand form a basic balancing feedback loop in the economy as a whole. When goods are scarce and demand is greater than supply, feedback works to reduce the demand in two ways – by increasing the price or by increasing the supply through sales and marketing. When supply is greater than demand, the loop works to increase demand by lowering the price, or reducing the supply through stockpiling or manufacturing cutbacks.

There are many balancing feedback loops that keep our environment steady. There is a natural ecology to a rainforest or prairie, coral reef, desert or marsh. Animals, plants and simpler organisms are tied together in complex interdependencies of feedback loops. They form a vast web, each maintaining its own life through its relationships with others. What may seem bad from one point of view is really necessary to preserve a balanced ecosystem. For example, occasional prairie fires are necessary. Fire hatches some sensitive seeds that would not otherwise blossom, it destroys the old, dry, decaying vegetation, it disposes of tree

saplings and keeps in check intruding plant species that are less
tolerant to fire. In the long term, fire revitalizes the prairies.
Ecologies seem to need a challenge to grow stronger.

Animals, too, need their predators to keep their numbers
steady. Predators and prey form a balancing feedback loop. For
example, Canadian wolves hunt moose, deer and caribou. During
a mild winter with a good food supply the deer increase. However,
their habitat cannot support the increase and after a while, they
begin to exhaust the food supply. As the population grows, so do
the numbers of old and sick deer. This is good news for the
wolves. The deer are plentiful and easier to catch, so the wolves
eat well for a time and grow fat. This reduces the number of deer
and soon only the fitter, faster deer are left. Now the tables are
turned, the wolves find it harder to hunt, the old and sick wolves
die sooner, and that takes the pressure off the deer. The environ-
mental food supply for the deer begins to replenish itself and the
cycle starts again. More deer means more wolves, which means
fewer deer, which means fewer wolves, which means more deer...
The wolves help to keep the deer population to what the environment can support and the deer return the compliment to the
wolves. That is the 'goal' of this particular system, although it is
not the goal of an individual deer, or individual wolf, were they
ever to think about it. It is hard on the individual animals, but it
keeps the total balance of nature so both species can survive.

When the natural balance is upset, both predators and prey
suffer. For example, the Kaibab plateau in Arizona can support
about 40,000 deer. Bounty hunters took a heavy toll of their
natural predators (wolves, cougars and coyotes), and the deer
population quickly climbed to beyond 50,000. There was not
enough food for them. In their desperation, the deer devoured
all available food, even stripping the bark from the trees. When
nothing was left, 40,000 deer starved.

Maybe illness is another example of balancing feedback. When we are tired or overworked, we are more likely to fall ill, then we have to rest for a few days, our body recovers and we cont-inue. Stress, which has been shown to make us more prone to illness, is one way the body signals the difference between its goal – our comfort zone – and our current situation. Illness forces us to take it easy for a few days and, hopefully, return to work more effectively afterwards. So some illness is (unwelcome) balancing feedback.

Healing is another example of balancing feedback. The body senses a difference between how it is and how it should be and acts to reduce the difference by clotting the blood to repair the injury, healing the wound, making scar tissue, or mobilizing the immune system to get rid of the offending antigen.

We could not survive or society or ecosystems function without balancing feedback loops. They are the glue that keep us all from falling apart.

Examples of Balancing Feedback

These are examples of balancing feedback loops. Some are very complex, containing many subsystems, but they all work overall as balancing feedback loops. Can you think of more?

Mechanical Systems

- car cruise control
- steam engine governor
- air conditioning

Human Systems

- body temperature
- hunger
- thirst
- pain
- blood sugar level
- blood pressure
- breathing
- illness
- coughing
- sleep
- healing
- writing
- painting
- driving a car
- riding a bicycle
- any action that involves trying to achieve a goal
- any other life-supporting functions

Ecological Systems

- predator and prey
- food and population balance

Social Systems

- elections
- market supply and demand
- income tax

Business

- customer care
- leadership
- managing inventory
- selling
- appraisal
- team building
- marketing

Feedforward – Back to the Future

Most of the time, feedback gives chains of cause and effect, where each action influences what follows. For example, thirst makes us drink and the drink causes us to feel less thirsty. In communication, what we say moulds the other person's reply and their reply sparks our response. A drop in temperature makes the thermostat turn on the furnace which leads to a rise in temperature which makes the thermostat turn off the furnace. Cause and effect go in circles and what was the cause from one point of view becomes the effect from the other.

The cause in the present gives rise to the effect in the future.

Feedforward describes an interesting and slightly different effect of some types of feedback. It comes from our ability to anticipate the future. It is when the anticipated effect in the future, which has not yet happened, triggers the cause in the present, which would otherwise not have happened. Thus the future reaches backwards to affect the present. For example, when you expect to fail, you often do. After all, what's the point in trying if it's a forlorn hope? When you expect to succeed, on the other hand, your energy and optimism help you and make it more likely that you will. Nothing succeeds like success. (And nothing fails like failure.)

Our hopes, fears and beliefs about the future help to create the very future we anticipate. So the best way to ensure a boring day out is to convince yourself in advance – expect the worst, rehearse it in your mind and pretend you know the future. Then because you 'know' it will be boring, you will daydream a lot and rush from one activity to another to get them over with as quickly as possible and be closer to going home. If you also constantly contrast whatever happens with another time that was so much better, you will ensure the day fully meets your expectations. To have an enjoyable day, do the opposite: anticipate it with pleasure, look forward to all the interesting things you will do, let it loom large and colourful in your mind. Enter into every activity fully. Sometimes we are pleasantly surprised (or unpleasantly disappointed), but generally speaking, the expectation of the event leads to the event you expect.

Feedforward creates self-fulfilling prophecies. In the stock market, the financial equivalent of 'nothing succeeds like success' is 'money attracts money'. Rumours circulate that a particular stock will rise. Although the stock has not risen, these rumours attract buyers. So the stock rises. The more it rises, the more buyers are attracted. A reinforcing loop is set up. Eventually stock market commentators start a balancing loop by saying the stock is overvalued and it falls as people sell.

Forecasts of short supply work in a similar way. Whenever a possible shortage is announced, what do people do? They go out and buy some of the commodity, 'just in case'. They even buy more than usual to tide them over the expected shortage, thus creating the very shortage they fear. When bakery workers went on strike some years ago, the small amount of bread made by the independent bakeries was quickly bought when the shops opened by people who had been queuing for up to three hours. When there was difficulty in getting petrol to petrol stations, we saw the ridiculous spectacle of cars queuing for hours to top up with a few litres, 'just in case' they couldn't get any more. This behaviour created a much more serious shortage than necessary. The smooth and continuous supply of petrol presupposes that not everyone has a full tank at any one time. We could manufacture a petrol crisis out of thin air if we all filled up our tanks at midday today. The supplies would be overstretched and there would be a shortage until the system adjusted to meet the new demand.

Money provides another example. If everyone withdrew their money from their bank account, the financial system would collapse. A rumour that a bank cannot meet its debts ensures the account holders will besiege the bank and withdraw their money. The bank does not carry enough money, creating a panic that can lead to the rumour becoming a fact. Which is the cause and which the effect? An impossible question as long as you think of causes and effects as separate and distinct.

A rumour may be completely unfounded, a prophecy may be a fake and the prophet a charlatan, but predictions can come true, not because they are a reasonable and accurate projections into the future, but because the very fact they have been made at all moulds the future. What matters is that people *believe and act* on the prophecy. Our beliefs shape our future.

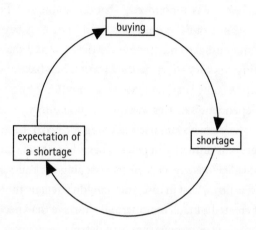

Feedforward

Occasionally feedforward has a novel twist. The very efforts a person takes to avoid something leads to – the event happening. This is like walking backwards into the hole you are trying to avoid. Joseph knows several people who have injured themselves playing squash because they were anxious about injury. Past injuries made them hesitant, so they held back on a stroke and put an unusual strain on their body, leading to a recurrence of the previous injury.

In the social sphere, a person may be anxious to make friends, so they make friendly overtures to nearly all the people they meet, but because their efforts have a slightly desperate, anxious quality, they put people off rather than draw people in.

Insomnia is a slightly different example. Suppose you are afraid you will not be able to sleep. You might *try* to go to sleep, but the harder you try, the more difficult it becomes. The more difficult it seems, the harder you try. Trying actually prevents sleep and reinforces the belief that falling asleep is hard. In the end, the only way to get to sleep is to stop trying.

This type of feedforward is at the heart of the 'Be spontaneous!' paradox. The more you try to do something that can only happen spontaneously, the less spontaneous you become. We can tie ourselves and others in knots by demanding behaviour that is only valuable if it is spontaneous.

Feedforward occasionally leads to self-defeating prophecies. Here an expectation or prediction about what will happen influences the present in such a way as to ensure the future state will not be reached. For example, telling a particularly determined athlete that they are going to lose can have the opposite effect. The more you tell them, the more determined they become to win; they go into the contest with extra energy and determination and that carries them to victory.

Summary of Feedback and Feedforward

- *Reinforcing feedback* is when the changes in the system are fed back and amplify the original change. In other words the 'effect' of the change reinforces the 'cause' to amplify the change. The system moves away ever faster from its initial point.
- This can lead to *reinforcing feedforward* when a prediction or anticipation drives the system away from the predicted state – a self-defeating prophecy.
- *Balancing feedback* is when the changes in the system feed back to oppose the original change and so dampen

the effect. In other words the 'effect' of the change opposes
the cause of the change. The system stabilizes towards a state
– its 'goal'.

■ *Balancing feedforward* is when the prediction or anticipation
of a change drives the system towards the predicted state.
These are the self-fulfilling prophecies.

When We Do Not Learn from Experience

We learn from experience by connecting cause and effect.
Touching a hot stove gives immediate feedback called pain and
we break the circle by withdrawing our hand fast. We learn that
touching the stove hurts and generalize that anything hot will
hurt, not just stoves. But suppose the pain and blister only
appeared two days later? Or a week later? Or a month? How
easy would it be to learn to avoid the hot plate? Food allergies
are notoriously difficult to pin down precisely because they do
not always happen immediately after eating the offending food.
Deep muscle pain usually appears one to two days after the
exertion that caused it. The side-effects of drugs can appear
months or years later. Advertising campaigns may take weeks
to change customers' buying patterns. We do our best to bring
up our children, but we have very little idea of how our actions
will influence them as adults.

The other part of learning from experience is *where* the feedback happens. It may be immediate, but if I do something here
and the effect is next door, I will not learn from it either. If the
sales division of a business gives away service to promote sales,
then the service department will suffer, but the feedback to the

sales department may be very favourable. The overburdened service department may be less impressed.

Feedback is a circle and it takes time to travel round a circle. This means that effects can appear some time after their cause. It is like what happens when we look at the stars. Because the stars are vast distances away, the light takes years to reach us. Even the light from the closest star, our sun, takes nine minutes to reach us. Look at a star tonight. You will not see it as it is now, but as it was many years ago. In a sense we are looking back in time.

Think of appetite as part of a feedback loop. The feedback is not so immediate as when we are thirsty. It is very unusual (and uncomfortable) to drink too much fluid, because we feel the effect on our thirst immediately. However, there is a time delay between the stomach being full and the sensation of satisfaction. When you digest food, sugars pass from the stomach into the blood and trigger the release of the neurotransmitter serotonin when they reach the brain. Serotonin stimulates another part of the brain to send the message that you are full. All this takes time. So the feeling of fullness is not directly related to how much food is in your stomach at that time, but to how much food was in your stomach several minutes ago. This delay between being full and the sensation of being full means you may continue to eat past the satisfied stage to the uncomfortable stage. If you are still eating when you feel full, you have gone too far. The way to avoid this is to eat more slowly, chewing well to speed the digestion of the sugars. Give yourself time for the feedback to appear.

When we do not take time delays into account we evaluate the success of our strategies too soon, long before the full consequences are observed. Then we may continue with a strategy, believing it effective, and not connect the eventual consequences with it, but put them down to other factors.

thinking in circles

The clearest example of time delays come from the effect of industrial chemicals on the environment. The first scientific papers suggesting that chlorofluorocarbons (CFCs) could destroy atmospheric ozone were published in 1974. It was not until 1985 that there was clear evidence of a deep hole in the ozone layer above the Antarctic. It takes 15 years for a CFC molecule released on the Earth's surface to make its way to the high stratosphere where it breaks down the protective ozone layer. The measurements in 1985 showed the effects of CFCs that were released in 1970. In 1990, 92 countries met in London and agreed to phase out all CFC production by the year 2000, but it will take over a century for the CFCs to be cleansed from the stratosphere.

We learn, then, from feedback that clearly connects effect and cause. When there is a long delay, we may think there is no effect at all and so learn nothing.

The more dynamically complex the system, the longer the feedback takes to travel around the network of connections. Some connections may be very fast, but it only takes one connection to slow the whole system down. One traffic jam can make you late, even when the other parts of the journey are fast. The speed of a system is determined by its slowest point. Sometimes this is not appreciated in business. Some procedures may become fully automated, but the overall production does not get any faster, because the real cause of the delay has not been addressed.

The time the feedback takes to go through the system and come back to you is the 'memory' of the system. It is the gap between cause and effect which you cannot see and so you do not know what is happening. For example, you once learned to read, but every time you read, it seems as though that skill comes from nowhere. Where does your reading skill go when you are not reading? Memory is not really a place, it is very difficult to pin down a definite part of the brain and say, 'That's where that piece of information is stored.' It is possible to stimulate specific memories by stimulating specific parts of the brain, but that does not mean they are stored there. You know you have remembered something when you use it later. Until then it is invisible, somehow held in the brain through the interconnection of the nerve cells.

When there is a time delay between cause and effect and we assume there is no effect at all, we may be surprised when the effect suddenly happens. And the effect will last as long as the cause that gave rise to it. Imagine a very long hose attached to a tap at one end. You turn on the tap and watch the other end of the hose. Nothing happens. So you turn the tap on more. Still nothing happens. You turn it on even more. Now water begins to flow out of the other end of the hose more and more strongly, even if you turn the tap off as soon as you see the water. The hose will gush water for as long as the tap was on, regardless of whether the tap is still on. The hose is the system and it 'remembers' what you did.

This time delay may fool us into adjusting too late and too much. Have you ever gone through the 'ordeal of ice and fire' with an unfamiliar shower? First thing in the morning, you stumble into the shower. The water becomes uncomfortably hot. You turn up the cold tap, but it gets hotter still. You turn up the cold even more. Then it cools down, but too much. It gets too chilly, so you quickly turn up the hot water again, only to be scalded a few moments later. The effect can be represented as shown in the graph overleaf.

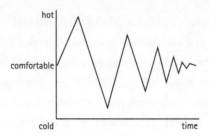

The ordeal of ice and fire

This is a classic pattern. It shows itself in market rises and falls, boom followed by collapse. It shows itself in cycles of inflation and deflation. Whenever you find a pattern like this in your life, you can be fairly sure it is caused by a balancing feedback loop with a time delay. One example would be being financially well off, spending freely, then suddenly finding you are broke and having to be extremely careful. The same pattern happens in business. In one quarter, cash is flowing freely, then suddenly a financial crisis looms. One moment a business is short of stock to cover customer orders, then a few weeks or months later is overstocked, for demand has dropped.

There are two solutions. One is to get more reliable measurements that give you more immediate feedback (change the plumbing of the shower to reduce the delay). Failing that, take the time delay into account and make the adjustment now that will lead you to being where you want to be when the change has taken its time working round the system. (Only turn the tap a little way and wait to feel the effect. This choice, however, may be uncomfortable in the short term.) The most important point is when you understand *how* something is happening, you are in a better position to do something about it.

In a very complex system, an effect may follow a very long time after its cause. By the time you see the effect it may have broached a critical threshold and it may be too late to reverse it. The effect of industrial chemicals on the environment shows this danger most clearly. PCBs (polychlorinated biphenyls) are chemicals that are used throughout the world in electrical equipment. They have been dumped in landfills and sewers for 40 years without a thought for the long-term consequences. A 1966 study that was originally designed to detect the pesticide DDT in the environment found PCBs to be widespread. PCBs move slowly through the soil and underground water. In the short term you might think that they have done no harm. However, the environment has them in its 'memory'. PCBs are fat soluble and once taken up into animal flesh, they accumulate in the body. They become more concentrated as they move up the food chain and are found in the greatest concentrations in sea birds, mammals and human breast milk. PCBs interfere with the human immune system and reproductive functions. Their production has been banned in most countries since the 1970s. However, 70 per cent of all PCBs ever produced are still in use or bound up in electrical equipment. The other 30 per cent have already been released into the environment. So far only 1 per cent has reached the oceans, where it is already measurable and having an effect on marine life. The remaining 29 per cent, still in the soil, lakes and rivers, are likely to be taken up by living creatures for decades or perhaps hundreds of years.

When you are dealing with systems, expect time delay. Do not expect to see the result of the change immediately.

What we do now will affect our lives in the future when the consequences come round again. If we do not see the connection, we may blame the prevailing conditions, when in fact the roots lie in our own past actions. We mould the future by what we do now.

Answers to the Exponential Growth Quiz

1 It would reach from the Earth to the moon if it were possible to fold it that many times.

2 You had better take action immediately because tomorrow it will cover the whole pond.

3 Most unwise. The twenty-first square is worth a million grains and there is not enough rice in the world to meet the debt on the sixty-fourth square. Checkmate.

---

1 Lutz, Dr W. *et al.*, *The Future Population of the World: What can we assume today?* Earthscan, 1996

What is a System?

A system is an entity that maintains its existence and functions as a whole through the interaction of its parts. The behaviour of different systems depends on how the parts are related, rather than on the parts themselves. Therefore you can understand many different systems using the same principles.

Systems form part of larger subsystems and are composed in turn of smaller systems.

The properties of a system are the properties of the whole. None of the parts has them. The more complex the system, the more unpredictable the whole system properties. These whole system properties are called *emergent properties* – they emerge when the whole system is working.

Breaking a whole into its parts is analysis. You gain knowledge by analysis. Building parts into wholes is synthesis. You gain understanding through synthesis. When you take a system apart and analyse it, it loses its properties. To understand systems you need to look at them as wholes.

Detail complexity means there is a great number of different parts.

Dynamic complexity means there is a great number of possible connections between the parts, because each part may have a number of different states.

Each part of a system may influence the whole system.

When you change one element, there are always side-effects.

Systems resist change because the parts are connected. However, when they do change, it can be sudden and dramatic. There will be particular places where you can effect large changes with very little effort once you understand the system. This is known as *leverage*.

Thinking in Circles

■ Systems thinking is thinking in circles rather than in straight lines. The connections between parts form feedback loops. Feedback is the output of a system re-entering as its input, or the return of information to influence the next step.

■ There are two types of feedback.

Reinforcing feedback is when changes in the system come back and amplify a change, leading to more change in the same direction. The system moves away ever faster from its initial point.

Reinforcing feedback can lead to runaway exponential growth.

Balancing feedback is when changes in the whole system feed back to oppose the original change and so dampen the effect. It leads to less of the action that is creating it. Balancing feedback keeps the system stable and resists attempts to change it.

■ All systems have a goal – even if that goal is only survival. The goal is its desired state, where the system is at rest or balanced. Balancing feedback acts to reduce the difference between where a system is and where it 'should' be. It drives the system towards a goal.

■ Feedforward is when prediction or anticipation of the future influences the present in a way that leads to a self-fulfilling or self-defeating prophecy.

■ Expect time delay between cause and effect in systems. The feedback loop takes time to complete. The more complex the system, the longer the feedback may take to appear. Time delays, if not taken into account, can lead to overshoot and oscillation.

making mental maps

3

mental models

Beliefs: Those things we hold to be true, despite evidence to the contrary.

Now we know what systems thinking is, we can relate it to the basic assumptions behind how we think and solve problems. A decision is only as good as the process used to produce it. Be ready to explore your own thinking with puzzles and illusions.

We will use systems thinking in four ways:

1 To solve problems directly. And not only solve them, but *eliminate the thinking that led to the problem in the first place.* Systems thinking is more than lateral thinking, it is vertical, horizontal, deep and circular thinking too.

2 To challenge, probe and clarify habitual ways of thinking.

3 To appreciate how our thinking is inseparable from the problems we encounter. Problems are not simply 'out there'. They are a co-creation of events and how we think about those events. We are the common element in all our problems and, as Einstein said, we cannot solve a problem with the same level of thinking that created it.

4 Lastly, you can gain more insight into your beliefs and ways of acting by applying systems thinking to your own system of thinking, because our beliefs are themselves a system.

We bring many deep-rooted assumptions, strategies, ways of looking and guiding ideas to whatever we do. These are known as *mental models* in systems thinking literature. Why mental models? 'Mental' because they exist in our minds and drive our actions, 'models' because we construct them from our experiences. They are our general ideas that shape our thoughts and actions and lead us to expect certain results. They are our theories in use, based mostly on observation and experience, but with a sprinkling of received wisdom and a dash of hope. They are what have worked in the past and therefore what we expect to work in the future. They are the maps we apply to our future explorations, drawn from our experience of what seemed successful on our past journey. They form our beliefs as we apply them to real life. We may not preach them, but we do practise them.

Mental models are quite natural, everyone has them, they are there whether we are aware of them or not, and we see the world through them. They are prized and personal. They are *ours*. We live inside them. The language we use about them is revealing. We talk of 'having' beliefs, of 'adopting' and 'acquiring' them. We say we 'hold' them, 'drop' them or 'abandon' them. We will 'defend' them from attack. When we 'lose' a belief it is usually gone for good and leaves a void that needs to be filled by another. Our mental models belong to us, but they do change and evolve with new experience, and we may need to refine them when we enter unfamiliar territory.

In short, our mental models guide all our actions. They provide stability, something to count on. We seek reinforcing feedback to confirm and reconfirm them, sometimes so insistently that we even welcome disaster as long as it corroborates our beliefs – the 'I told you so' scenario.

So our mental models give meaning to events. We interpret our experience in the light of them. They are not *facts*, although we sometimes take them to be so. For example, we agree on the basic physical properties of matter as far as they affect us. Qualities like mass and volume are known as first order properties. To these first order properties, each of us adds *meaning* – second order properties. A ring made of metal has some obvious first order properties, as any metallurgist will tell you. However, if it is a wedding ring, it has personal value and significance that far outweigh those physical properties. There is a passage in the film *Raiders of the Lost Ark* where Indiana Jones, the archaeologist hero, confronts his enemy Belloc in a café in Cairo. 'Look at this watch,' says Belloc. 'To you and I it is worthless, but bury it in the sand for 1,000 years and it becomes priceless. Men will kill for it...' A lump of metal can become an archaeological treasure.

Our mental models are deep rooted and they predispose us to experience in a particular way. We use them to discriminate and decide what is important and what is not. We may then mistake our view for reality, we mistake the map for the ground it represents. You can see this for yourself by looking at the next diagram. It is a figure called a Kanizsa triangle, named after the psychologist Gaetano Kanizsa. What do you see?

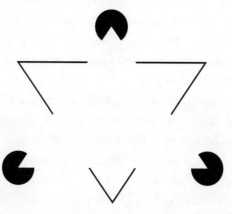

Kanizsa triangle

There is no white triangle, but the illusion is compelling. Why? Our eyes do not work like a camera, objectively recording the world. They work with the brain to interpret shapes in a certain way. So what we are aware of seeing is created by how our eyes work, as well as what is 'out there'. In the same way our mental models shape what we see, hear and feel. It is hard to examine our mental models, just as it is hard to see how the eye works. Our biases seem to be really 'out there', just like the ghostly Kanizsa triangle. We can know our biases by examining what we do and how we react, and deducing our assumptions about what we experience.

Mental models are like the filters in the eye and brain that create the Kanizsa triangle, but whereas the filters are built into our physiology and are therefore unchangeable, *we can change our mental models*.

How We Make our Mental Models

Given we all have mental models, how did we build them? A baby does not arrive with a built-in set of beliefs, but with the capability to construct them. Different people can have the same experience, yet explain it in very different ways and read very different meanings into it.

We make our mental models partly from our social mores, partly from our culture and partly from the ideas of significant adults in our childhood. The rest we construct and maintain from our experience of life in four main ways:

DELETION

We are selective about what we notice. Every waking moment, our senses are being stimulated and there is no way we could notice and deal with all the possible information. So we select and filter according to our moods, interests, preoccupations and general alertness.

Try this experiment. Look at the black dot below with both eyes from about 6 inches (15 centimetres) away. Now close your right eye and look straight at the black dot with your left eye. *Keep staring straight ahead* and slowly move the page to your left. At one point, the spot will disappear, because the image is falling on the blind spot in your left eye, where the optic nerve enters the retina from the brain, so there are no light-sensitive cells to receive the image.

●

The blind spot

We delete information and form our ideas from what we notice. There is always other information, but it carries no significance for us, so for all intents and purposes it is not there. Deletion also maintains our mental models once they are formed. For example, parents often simply do not notice that their child has grown up – they continue to see them as a child, and are blind to their increasing independence and maturity until it suddenly seems to happen all at once. (Sometimes with explosive results!)

CONSTRUCTION

Construction is the mirror image of deletion: we see something that is not there. Seeing is believing. Look at the next diagram. Hold the book about 12 inches (30 centimetres) away, focus on the small cross on the right and then close your right eye. Now, keep focusing on the cross and move the book slowly towards you. After a few inches, not only will the circle disappear, but you will also find the middle horizontal line looks unbroken. Your brain has filled in the gap. This is also the reason why you do not see a 'hole' in your visual field caused by the blind spot. We fill in the gaps so the world makes sense and appears how we think it ought to be.

We have a lovely example from researching this book. Later in this chapter there is some quoted research from a psychologist named Wason. When we looked up the original research, we mis-read the name as 'Watson' several times because that is what was expected – it is a much more usual name. Seeing 'Wason' in the index of another book, we assumed they had made an error! It was only noticing 'Wason' in the index of yet another book that we started to doubt our version and double checked all the references.

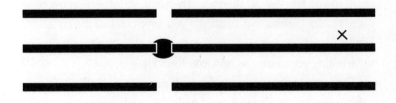

mental models

Ambiguity is almost guaranteed to induce construction. We read ambiguity like a fortune-teller's tea leaves, finding patterns and significance in the most obscure or random events. Indeed, one of our strongest mental models, and a very useful one, is that there is pattern and sense to the world, only sometimes we jump at it too soon or create one that is not there. A resolution – any resolution – seems preferable to continued ambiguity.

The interesting series of experiments conducted by the psychologist John Wright in 1960 is a nice example of construction.[1] Volunteers played a machine similar to a one-armed bandit. There were 16 identical small buttons and a counter. The object of the game (we abbreviate the experiment a great deal in this description) was to gain as high a score as possible by pushing a sequence of buttons in the correct order. The subjects had no clues and were given no rules about the sequence, except they were told a buzzer would sound when they succeeded in getting the correct order. So they tried to get the buzzer to sound as many times as possible.

Imagine for a moment you are a subject in this experiment. You sit in front of the machine and you have to rely on your memory because you are not allowed to keep written notes. There are 13 trials, each consisting of 25 attempts. During the first 10 trials, you experiment with various combinations and get about half of them right. Then for two trials you do not get any right, so you revise your theories. After that, you are right every time. You feel proud and satisfied – you have cracked the code. You backtrack in your mind and get ready to tell the experimenter the winning sequence and how you found it.

Then the experimenter confounds you – the whole experiment was a set up. For the first 10 blocks, the buzzer was pre-set to sound 50 per cent of the time at random intervals. Then two trials of silence, regardless of what you did. For the last 10, it was pre-set to sound every time. In other words, there was no connection between what you did and your success or failure as signalled by the buzzer. Many subjects in this experiment were so sure they had discovered the sequence, they did not see how it could have been random. It fitted in with their strategy so perfectly that they thought the experimenter was lying.

The experiment shows how easy it is to construct plausible explanations and mistake the connections we make with the actual events. With the benefit of hindsight, everything is rational. And we tend to link probable cause with possible effect, smoothing the rough edges of a story we want to be true.

DISTORTION

Distortion is how we change our experience, amplifying some parts and diminishing others. It is the basis of creativity as well as paranoia. Again, we have a visual analogy. Look at the next diagram.

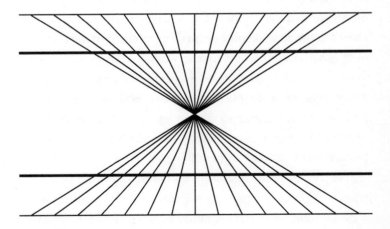

Hering figure

mental models

This is known as the Hering figure; the horizontal lines look tilted, but they are not.

When we distort events, we give more weight to some experiences than others. It is not a bad thing to do, but it can lead us astray. It is all too easy to reclassify experiences to back up preconceived ideas. For example, many gamblers continue to believe that they can and will win despite the fact they keep losing. They do so by reframing losses as 'near wins'.

Jealousy is a good example of how distortion can be limiting and painful. A jealous person can distort all sorts of everyday, innocent events into suspicious, threatening and painful possibilities.

GENERALIZATION

Using generalization, we create our mental models by taking one experience and making it represent a group. For example, a child sees how their parents treat each other and generalizes to make a mental model of how men and women treat each other. Generalization is a basic part of how we learn and apply our knowledge in different situations. We recognize something we already know, so we know how to deal with it. Without the ability to generalize, we would have to work out every problem from scratch. Whenever we use words like 'always', 'never', 'all', 'everybody' and 'nobody', we are generalizing.

The danger is to take an unrepresentative example, generalize to many other similar examples and then become blinkered to any evidence to the contrary. For example, a manager may believe consultants are useless in his industry, because he has generalized from one bad experience with a consultant. This generalization has to be maintained by deleting all the examples where consultants have done good work and made a difference.

Generalization combined with prejudice is an unpleasant mix. It is the basis of all racial and sexual discrimination.

These four principles of deletion, construction, distortion and generalization are not bad in themselves – they are the basis of our learning, creativity and all our beliefs, including the ones that serve us well. From a systems viewpoint, we want to know how these four principles combine to make the reinforcing and stabilizing loops that keep our belief system in place. Then we can see where they limit us and how we can expand our thinking.

Mental Models as a System

Mental models form a system. All systems have a purpose. The purpose of your belief system is to explain and give meaning to your experience, and looked at *from this point of view only* it does not have to provide you with a healthy or happy life. It is possible to have many beliefs about yourself and others that are limiting and unrealistic. But it is in our power to examine and recreate our belief system. We want a set of mental models that are realistic and useful, and provide ourselves and others with the greatest possible happiness and well-being. We can do this by looking dispassionately at our mental models, seeing them as a system and choosing what models to adopt, rather than holding those we already have regardless.

This suggests three courses of action:

■ Look and question how you gather reinforcing feedback that strengthens existing beliefs and how balancing feedback between your mental models keeps the whole system from changing.

■ Define the qualities of mental models you want – those that are realistic, and give you and others the greatest possible health and well-being.

■ Gather balancing feedback based on your goal of building realistic mental models that give the greatest possible health and well-being. Then your new experiences will affect and update your mental models.

There are three main factors that can cause us to misinterpret our experience so that it seems to provide reinforcing feedback that strengthens our existing mental models – regression, time focus and one-sided events.

REGRESSION

Regression is a statistical principle that can lead to mistaking a connection for a cause. Generalizing from this will make it worse. For example, suppose today is exceptionally sunny and hot. What are the chances of tomorrow being equally hot? Not so good. The more extreme one event, the more likely the next will be closer to the average. Any extreme experience is more likely to be followed by one that is closer to average, otherwise over the long term, the extreme would become the average. Very bad weather is likely to be followed by better weather. Very tall parents tend to have less tall children. A poor business performance will probably pick up given time. A superb success is likely to be followed by something more mundane.

Now, suppose you did some weather magic, believing that you could influence the weather to be cooler tomorrow. Would cooler weather tomorrow prove your magic was effective? No. It is much more likely to be due to the principle of regression.

Because events tend to regress towards their average value, it is dicey to predict on the basis of exceptional events. Many a business has been lost and many a poor investment made through not taking this principle into account.

Regression is a statistical fact of life, but instead of taking it into account, it is tempting to make up complicated theories to account for events. But beware of a prediction or explanation based on an unusually good or bad result, especially if it confirms your beliefs. For example, a poor performance is usually followed by a better one without a reward as a motivation to do better or a punishment as a deterrent for slacking. What is taken for evidence for the efficacy of rewards and punishments is mostly due to the regression principle. A poor sales month is usually followed by a better one, but the improvement may be put down to a new training course or bonus scheme. We construct an explanation that is not warranted by the facts or use regression as evidence that our actions have the desired effect and thereby confirm our mental models.

TIME FOCUS

Events are often mistaken as reinforcing feedback because no time limits have been set. In other words, we do A and expect B to happen. Whenever B happens, whether it be hours, days, weeks, months or even years afterwards, we take it as the effect of A and as proof of the connection. This evidence is not *focused in time*. (This is quite different from analysing a system in the present and predicting a time lag between cause and effect where the time lag can often be accurately predicted.)

Here is a typical example of unfocused evidence. Many managers believe that people can be motivated to work creatively by financial rewards. It is easy to get evidence for this belief – reward someone and then wait for the creative work. Whenever it happens, whether today, tomorrow or in a month's time, it can be used as evidence to confirm the belief. If it does take some time, then a handy back-up belief is something like, 'It takes time for people to see their own best interests.' The regression principle almost guarantees they will come up with creative work sometime in the future and it will not necessarily be connected to the reward. In fact there is considerable evidence that rewards are motivating only on very limited occasions.[2] Twenty-five years of research has produced no evidence that people work any more productively when they are expecting a reward than when they expect to be equally rewarded or on the basis of need.[3] The exception is when the task is very easy and not very interesting, i.e. when there is no intrinsic reward in the task itself.

It is much safer to make evidence time focused, in other words look for evidence within a specific time, then the result will be memorable and significant whether it confirms your belief or not.

ONE-SIDED AND TWO-SIDED EXPERIENCES

When you have no time focus, you only notice confirming evidence that provides reinforcing feedback for your beliefs. This means you have set up a one-sided experience – only one result is significant and noteworthy. For example, a manager may be really enthusiastic about a new advertising campaign. When sales eventually pick up, they are pleased and remember the upturn. Memory comes from attention in the past tense.

Does it seem as though you always need to stop for petrol when you are in a hurry? Or the telephone always rings when you are in the bath? It's the same effect at work. You remember the times it happened, but not all the times it did not, because those were non-events. A person who only looks for evidence in one-sided experiences is the sort of person who will wonder why someone always answers the telephone when they dial a wrong number!

Two-sided experiences are those that are memorable regardless of what happened, favourable or unfavourable. Going on a date, taking a holiday or gambling on the stock market are all two-sided events. All the possible outcomes evoke the same intensity of emotion, or even the same emotion.

It is still possible to back up mental models from two-sided experiences by justifying any result that did not confirm your mental model. For example, our manager who firmly believes in their advertising campaign may explain away a downturn in sales that is too big to ignore by attributing it to external difficulties, economic factors or the campaign not being done quite right, but next time...

■ *One-sided, unfocused experiences* will always provide rein-forcing feedback for existing beliefs. There is no possibility of balancing feedback, so no possibility of new information. You wait for as long as it takes to confirm your idea.

An example of a mental model that sets up one-sided, unfocused experiences is: 'People will only change when they are ready.'

■ *One-sided, focused experiences* can also confirm exist-ing mental models. One example would be looking for an upturn in sales in the next quarter due to a new

---

incentive scheme. If the result does occur within the time frame, then that is taken as evidence for the incentive scheme. If it does not occur, then it may be explained away, leaving the mental model intact. Sometimes the time focus gets a bit blurry and elastic...

■ *Two-sided, unfocused experiences* are generated by our long-term strategies. Both outcomes are significant, but hard to evaluate because there is no time limit on when they occur. An example is a man applying for work. The result of any one application is important – success or failure – but the effectiveness of his strategy is hard to gauge because he will keep trying until he is successful.

■ *Two-sided, focused experiences* provide the most valuable feedback for our mental models. We pay attention to all the possibilities within a time limit. When predicted effect follows cause, we can have some confidence in the result as reinforcing feedback, provided we have taken regression into account. If our prediction does not materialize, then this is also significant and becomes useful balancing feedback that casts doubt on the belief.

Self-fulfilling prophecies (balancing feedforward), where the prediction or anticipation of change drives the system towards its predicted state, relies mostly on unfocused, one-sided experience as evidence for the predicted outcome.

What can we learn about our mental models from our experiences?

■ Unfocused experiences are little use in telling us whether our mental models are accurate. Useful feedback should be time focused.

■ Two-sided experiences provide the most useful feedback.

Ask this key question when an experience seems to confirm a mental model: 'If the exact opposite happened, would I take that as also confirming my mental model?' If the answer is yes, then you have set up your experience so that you cannot get good feedback on your ideas.

This does not mean you should try to set up all your evidence in a two-sided focused way. It is just not possible. It does, however, mean that you should be careful about taking one-sided, unfocused experiences as evidence for your mental models, because they are not reliable.

We need to be scientists of our mental models. Scientists learn from their experiments however they turn out. Experiments that fail are the most valuable, because they show something has been overlooked – there is something to be learned, the model is not completely accurate. Experiences that contradict our mental models provide valuable balancing feedback if you pay attention to them. Whenever there is a discrepancy between what we expect and what happens, seize the opportunity. Become curious. What are you missing?

In general, we pay too much attention to experience that provides reinforcing feedback. We ask questions of our experience designed to get a 'yes' response. When events reinforce our beliefs we tend to ask ourselves, '*Can* I believe that?' And when events do not back up our beliefs we ask ourselves, '*Must* I believe that?' One word changed that makes a great deal of difference to our inner experience. Say both phrases to yourself, one after the other, and notice the different effect each has on your internal state.

Fruitful Thinking

Here is a puzzle. To solve it, you will have to think about what your choice tells you and also what your choice rules out. (Hint.)

Three closed boxes are labelled 'Apples', 'Oranges' and 'Apples and Oranges'. Each label is incorrect. You may examine only one fruit from each box (and no feeling around allowed!) How many fruits must you examine in order to label each box correctly?

The answer is on page 80.

You can use the next puzzle to test your tendency to pay too much attention to confirming feedback. Try it on your friends too.

Here is a set of four cards. Each has a letter on one side and a number on the other. You can only see one side of each card.

What is the least number of cards you need to turn over to test the rule that vowels always have an even number on the other side? Think about it for a moment.

E   G   4   9

In research on these sorts of tests[4] fewer than 5 per cent of people gave the correct answer – turn over the 'E' card and the '9' card. The rule says a vowel must pair with an even number, therefore you must turn over the vowel card – 'E'. If there is an odd number on the other side, then the rule is broken. The 'G' card is irrelevant, whatever is on the back. The '4' card is also irrelevant because the rule does not say that even numbers have to have vowels on the back. This card only confirms what you already know from turning over the 'E' card. The '9' card must be examined, because if it has a vowel on the back then it breaks the rule.

Challenging Mental Models

Systems thinking challenges many of our mental models. First it challenges the idea that the whole is the sum of its parts. People in difficult family relationships often think that if only one other person would change, then everything would be fine and go back to normal. It wouldn't. A balanced family is the result of *all* the relationships in it. Our health depends on all our bodily systems working together. A business team or a sports team, when it truly works together, will get results far beyond what the collection of individuals could achieve, and conversely, a team of very talented individuals may underachieve, because they do not know how to work well together. Team building is not simply a matter of throwing together all the best people. That is often a disaster because they are incompatible.

Secondly, systems thinking challenges the idea that you can judge a person's behaviour independent of the system they are in. A fundamental principle of systems thinking is that the structure of a system gives rise to its behaviour. Given favourable circumstances, anyone can shine, but we still blame and reward people as if they were independent entities, especially in the business world. A manager may be blamed for not acting correctly when in fact they were prevented from getting the information they needed because of a procedure in another department. If our mythical manager decides to play a blame game, then they may blame the other department for being slow. That department can then blame the method of collecting the data, which may have been agreed by everyone, including the original manager. Blame dissolves within a system. So when you point the finger of blame in a system you will end up pointing it back at yourself as well as everyone else because of the feedback loops and circles of cause and effect. No one comes to work to do a bad job, but the structure of the system may make good work impossible. If management falls into the blame trap, they may fire the offending individual and hire someone else – who may do no better. Rather than trying to find extraordinary people to do a job, design the job so that ordinary people can do it well. It is the structure of the system that creates the results. For better results, change the structure of the system.

Finally, systems thinking challenges us to rethink our ideas of cause and effect...

Answer to the Three Boxes Puzzle

Pick a fruit from the box labelled 'Apples and Oranges'.
Suppose it turns out to be an apple. What can you say about what is in the box? Not much directly, but you know the box is not 'Apples and Oranges' because all boxes are wrongly labelled.

You know it is not 'Apples' because that would not contain an orange. Therefore it must be oranges. You know all the boxes are wrongly labelled, so switch the labels of the other two boxes and you have the answer.

---

1 Wright, John, 'Consistency and complexity of response sequences', *Journal of Experimental Psychology* 63 (1962): 601–9

2 McGraw, Kenneth, 'The detrimental effects of reward on performance' in M. Lepper and D. Greene (eds.), *The Hidden Costs of Rewards*, Earlbaum, 1978

3 Deutsch, Morton, *Distributive Justice: A social-psychological perspective*, Yale University Press, 1985

4 Wason, P., and Johnson-Laird, P., *Psychology of Reasoning: Structure and content*, Harvard University Press, 1972

cause and effect

Cause and effect may seem straightforward. When cause A happens, effect B follows. And if B happens, that means A has happened. Doesn't it?

As we've already seen, it's not quite that simple. Let's take an obvious and undisputed example of cause and effect. Surely gravity causes objects to fall? However, like all physical laws, it has the unwritten proviso *everything else being equal*. So a feather would not fall in a strong wind, nor an iron bar in a strong magnetic field. (And even something as obvious as the force of gravity depends on the distance between the objects, in other words the relationship between them, so systems thinking must apply there too.) Or take the example of the virus that 'causes' the common cold. Ten people can be exposed to the virus and only one may come down with a cold – the person must somehow have been predisposed, so everything else was not equal. Even physical laws depend on a whole network of influencing factors.

When we think of a cause leading to an effect with everything else being equal, that 'everything else' is actually the larger system that contains the piece you are looking at. The laws of physics, for example, are idealized. They are seen as universal and applicable everywhere, but really they are applicable in their pure form nowhere except in an artificial experimental environment! They do not take into account the context, the environment or the system of influences that surround them. Reality is a lot more complicated than it may seem.

When we come to other types of cause and effect, for example, fast driving 'causes' accidents or unemployment 'causes' crime, the link is even more complex and arguable. There are other, complicating factors involved. We use the same word, 'cause', but these two examples do not depend on any law of physics or logic. We make up causal theories all the time: more police means less crime, more money means a happier life, seat belts save lives or computers make work quicker. They are all debatable. They may be true in the majority of cases, but it is impossible to say they are true with conviction in any *individual* case. Even when we say, 'Cigarette smoking causes lung cancer,' it means there is a very strong statistical link between cigarette smoking and lung cancer, but it is not the single cause, otherwise everyone who smoked would get lung cancer, and they do not. Smoking is one important factor – again, with everything else being equal.

When we are asked to answer a difficult question like 'What causes crime?' we tend to generate a list of factors like poor education, unemployment, law and order policy, housing conditions, opportunity and breakdown of values. We also tend to weigh each factor on the list from the most important to the least important. This has been called 'laundry list thinking'.[1] It assumes a one-way passage of influence from cause to effect and each factor has a fixed relative importance. Systems thinking goes far beyond laundry list thinking by showing circles of influence and that the relative importance of each factor may well change over time, depending on the feedback loops. Causes are dynamic, not static.

It makes more sense to think about *influencing factors* rather than causes. In systems thinking, it is the relationship between the elements that makes them into a cause or an effect. And that relationship depends on the structure of the system.

Ultimately, causes lie in the structure of the system.

Take population increase as an example. Birth rates cause the population to rise, death rates cause a decline, so it is possible to have a positive birth rate but a declining population, if the death rate is greater. So what causes the population to rise is neither one factor nor the other, but the relationship between them.

Finally, do not mistake the leverage point as the cause. We know that we can get a big shift if we change the right element, but that does not mean that element was the cause of the trouble, only that changing it was the easiest way to change the structure of the system because of the knock-on effect.

Three Fallacies

Systems thinking highlights three fallacies of cause and effect:

1. CAUSE AND EFFECT ARE SEPARATE AND THE EFFECT COMES AFTER THE CAUSE.

Cause and effect are different words, but depending on your point of view, they may refer to the same event. Feedforward demonstrates how the effect of a cause can be the cause of an effect. Does the shortage cause the hoarding or the hoarding cause the shortage? It is an impossible question because we are dealing with circles – go along the line for long enough and you will come back to where you started. Which one comes first depends on where you start. We are used to thinking in terms of either cause *or* effect. In systems it can be both.

2. EFFECT FOLLOWS CAUSE CLOSELY IN TIME AND SPACE.

We expect this, and when effect does closely follow cause, it is easier to connect the two, but it is not true in systems. In systems there are always delays and an effect may appear in a different part of the system. So when we deal with systems we have to extend our time horizon and look further afield for cause and effect chains.

Referred pain is an example. Trouble in a part of the body that does not have pain receptors appears as pain in a different part of the body. Heart trouble is often heralded by pains in the left arm. A trapped nerve in the back can cause pains down the leg. The effects of injury in one part of the body can lead to pain in another. An osteopath we know told us about one of her patients with severe neck pain. Treating the neck directly had no effect and it took a few weeks to get to the bottom of the trouble. The patient had hurt her right big toe. This caused her to walk a little awkwardly, shifting the weight from her painful foot, and this put a slightly different strain on her pelvis. The muscle groups in her back and neck tightened to compensate, and this muscle tightening led to the neck pain.

So, looking for the effect close to the cause can lead us to false conclusions. We may also be misled by plausible explanations because we tend to look for events that prove our preexisting mental models. Remember that in systems thinking the explanation does not lie in different single causes, but in the *structure* of the system and the relationships within it.

Be particularly careful when you see a repeated pattern. Look for the cause in the *pattern*, not in the different explanations on each occasion, especially if they involve blaming external factors. Repetition is a clue to an underlying systems structure:

■ Once is an event.
■ Twice is noteworthy.
■ Three times is a pattern – it will lead you to the systems structure.

One man we know seemed to have appalling luck with his car. He was involved in three accidents in a year and was not even in the car at the time. Other cars just kept running into it. He lived in a residential road and parked his car outside his house. In the first accident, a drunken driver hit the front of his car one evening. Two months later, a sober driver was distracted by a dog running across the road and scraped his car. The third time the car was hit was in heavy rain. Each accident was unique.

The drink, the dog and the rain were certainly important, precipitating causes, but our friend was tempting fate. He insisted on parking right outside his house and this meant parking on the wrong side of the road a few yards from a fairly sharp bend that fed into a much faster road. After the third debacle, and a letter from his insurance company, he parked much further up the road and has been accident free since then.

Now suppose we take the example of a business that regularly misses its sales targets. Maybe the first quarter's figures are adequately explained by the slow post-Christmas market. The poor second quarter is put down to economic factors beyond the company's control. The third quarter was bad because the top salesperson left and the fourth quarter was Christmas, so there was a lot of competition. But the figures will remain bad until the management addresses the underlying factors. To do this they will need to look at the business as a system. The cause could be a combination of low staff morale, inadequate customer service and poor recruitment procedures. The targets may be unrealistically high, but are set high to finance a high borrowing requirement. With systems thinking you can look beyond surface events, however tempting, to the deeper factors that are causing the pattern.

3. THE EFFECT IS PROPORTIONAL TO THE CAUSE.

This idea is true of physical objects – when one car hits another, the damage and the impact depend on the mass and velocity of the cars – but it cannot be generalized to living or mechanical systems. In mechanical systems, you can get a big effect from a small input, like a surge of power when you put your foot on the accelerator of a car, because the system can amplify the effects with reinforcing loops. Cause and effect are even more uncertain in living systems. A huge epidemic can be caused by something as small as a virus. Introducing a single pesticide can have widespread effects on the ecological balance of a region. If you hit a living creature it may run away or turn around and bite you. The energy for the response (the 'effect') comes not from your force but from within the creature and is known as *collateral energy*. It was there before your action (the 'cause').

Sometimes an action has no effect at all, because systems have thresholds. When the stimulus is below the threshold, nothing happens. Once it reaches the threshold, you get the complete response. The animal will not half bite you, depending on how hard you hit it. The response does not vary in proportion to the input.

Conventional physics deals with closed systems, those that can be considered isolated from their environment. In a closed system, the final state is completely determined by the initial conditions. A thermostat is a closed system. Given a temperature setting, you can predict its behaviour. Social systems and living systems are open systems – they maintain themselves from moment to moment by taking in and giving out to the surrounding environment. We take in oxygen and food to maintain ourselves and give out carbon dioxide and waste to the environment. We change constantly in order to stay the same. We do not suffer the same wear and tear as a closed system, we can heal ourselves. One year hence, your appearance will be much the same, yet over 90 per cent of the atoms in your body will be different.

Open systems are extremely sensitive to starting conditions. One morning a traffic jam may not disturb you at all. The next morning a similar jam will be incredibly frustrating. Your reaction will depend on how you felt at the beginning. This is what makes living systems so unpredictable. A very small difference in starting conditions can lead to a very different result given the same stimulus. This is the starting-point for the science of chaos that looks at the behaviour of complex systems.

The Two Sides of Chaos

Chaos and the sensitivity of complex systems to initial conditions are exemplified in the so-called 'butterfly effect', named after a talk given by the meteorologist Edward Lorenz at the Massachusetts Institute of Technology. Its title was 'Does the flap of a butterfly's wings in Brazil set off a tornado in Texas?' The talk came out of his research in 1961, examining computer models of weather patterns. On one occasion, he wanted to examine a sequence at greater length and instead of starting the computer run from the beginning, started it halfway through, typing in the initial conditions from the earlier print-out. When he returned later, the new print-out, which he expected to be exactly the same as the old, was wildly different. Lorenz had rounded up the initial numbers when he typed them in. He had typed in three decimal places instead of six, assuming that the difference was so small as to be inconsequential. The simulation proved that in a complex system such as the weather, a tiny initial change can be magnified into a completely different pattern over time. Short-range weather forecasts are usually reasonable accurate. Long-range forecasts are much riskier.

We can see the same forces at work in the small, seemingly random events that shape our lives. There are many science fiction stories (including the *Back to the Future* films) that play on how life would be different if some small event had not taken place. And small events can have large consequences. A chance telephone call can lead to a meeting that starts you on a new career path. A few words spoken in jest can change your life. And we can never hit the replay button and see how it might have been. We create our future from the small, seemingly unimportant decisions we make every day and we only know which were important when we look back later.

Chaos theory also has a flip side. Events that seem random may have some hidden order if you know where to look. If you take a simple system and apply the same simple change over and over again, it can become very complex indeed. Chaos is not random. The same pattern may be repeated, however deeply you look. For example, the pattern you see when you look at a coastline from the air is very like the pattern you see of a smaller piece of coastline from the ground and the same again when you look even closer. It never smoothes itself out; the pattern is an emergent. These patterns that are repeated at every level are called *fractals*.

There is an apocryphal story of the American psychologist William James fielding a question and answer session at the end of a public lecture on religion and cosmology at Harvard University. Asked by a member of the audience what keeps the Earth from falling through space, he thought it wisest first to ask his questioner their thoughts on the matter.

'That's easy,' said the enquirer. 'The world is resting on the back of a giant turtle.'

James asked the obvious question. 'But what stops the turtle from falling?'

'You can't catch me with that,' came the reply. 'It's turtles all the way down!'

Chaos theory is fractals all the way down.

We do not usually create a new branch of science without someone trying to make money out of it and chaos theory is no exception. The stock exchange is a very complex system and the holy grail for financially minded chaos scientists is some pattern, some fleeting order in the seemingly random fluctuations of the prices from day to day, week to week, that they can pounce on and use to make their fortune. In 1996, a physicist who had created a computer model of the flow of crowds in a confined space found that when he ran the program substituting the ebb and flow of currency prices produced by the interactions of thousands of traders the world over for the ebb and flow of the crowds, he was able to predict some trends in the dollar-yen exchange rate a month in advance. The movement of crowds and currency seem to share some of the same patterns. But before we celebrate the wealth that might be made from such a program if it were made more precise, we might, as systems thinkers, ask what would be the reinforcing feedforward consequences? If the stock market were predictable, how would that predictability change its behaviour so that in effect it would become unpredictable again?

There may be two kinds of complexity: inherent and apparent. Inherent complexity is the real thing, the dark side of chaos. Small variations at the beginning make huge differences as time goes by, the feedback loops form such a tangle that the whole system is a Gordian knot and not even the most powerful computer could come up with the sword of Damocles to cut it. Apparent complexity is the light side of chaos – it looks complicated, but there is order in there, even sometimes quite simple patterns. As systems thinkers, we are looking for the patterns in apparent complexity. High inherent complexity is the realm of the Cray super-computers and chaos theorists. It is fascinating territory, but this book will not attempt to map it. Low complexity, and apparent to boot, is the home of the easy problems. We are interested in the middle ground, where apparent complexity is high, but real, and inherent complexity is low.

There are two ideas that help to understand and limit complexity in a system. First, establish useful boundaries. So if you are looking at your finances, on one side you can safely exclude the molecular structure of the coins and notes, and the holographic structure of the image on your credit card. On the other side you can also exclude how your spending pattern fits into the projected national figures for fiscal flow in the present financial year. However, your state of

health, goals and dreams for the future may well be relevant.
You decide the boundaries. The wider you cast your net, the
more complexity there will be.

Like us, you may have done some DIY house improvements.
Perhaps you needed to wallpaper a room. While you are moving the furniture, you decide to replace some old chairs. And
stripping the wallpaper would be a good opportunity to replace
the light rose on the ceiling and the light switch on the wall that
are looking decidedly grubby. Maybe a dimmer switch would be
nice... When you start that, you realize the wiring is rather old
and could really do with being replaced. Might as well do the
whole lighting circuit, it would save money... That would mean
taking up the floorboards. So it would be a good opportunity to
replace some carpets... Before you know it, your simple DIY job
can make you seriously consider moving house unless you
define the boundaries.

Complex systems can revert to stable patterns. Imagine turning on a tap. Just a little. The water drips out in a regular way.
Keep turning, and suddenly the drips coalesce and the water
flows out in a chaotic, turbulent pattern. You have hit a threshold.
Keep turning and you will get a different pattern again – the
water will gush out like a torrent. Now what would happen if
you could get the tap to just the point between one water pattern
and the next? It couldn't stay there. It would fall to one side or
the other, behaving like a ball balanced on the top of a hill.
Complex systems seem to want to revert to some stable state.
These are called *attractors* in self-organization theory – that
part of chaos theory that deals with how order seems to arise
spontaneously in complex systems, like a snowflake forming in
the atmosphere or a crystal suddenly precipitating from a liquid.
We know snowflakes will form given the right atmospheric
conditions, but we cannot predict the form of any one snow-

flake. These ordered states are emergents and happen from the particular organization of feedback in the system. We all have particular ways of perceiving and understanding events. For example, look at the diagram.

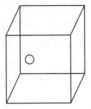

Attractor states

Is the face of the cube marked with the small circle at the front or at the back? Sometimes you see it at the front, then it flips to the back. Both views are steady, but trying to see it in between is like trying to keep the tap balanced at the point between two different flow patterns of water – it goes to one or the other.

The implications are fascinating. On the social level, it is arguable that democracy is an attractor once a social system grows to a certain level of complexity. Other types of political organization are not stable enough. On the business level, organizations will settle into particular stable states. As a ball rolls down a slope into a valley, so these attractors are easy to slide into, but take a lot of pushing to get out of. Sometimes change management is like the labour of Sisyphus, who in Greek mythology was condemned forever to push a large rock to the top of a hill only to have it roll back down to the bottom at the last moment. However, once you make it to the top of the hill, change can be surprisingly quick.

Organizational change first involves destabilizing the system in its present state and then creating another attractor state,

cause and effect

which must involve not only a business structure and procedures but also a vision and values.

At an individual level, we may have personal equivalents of attractor states. You are likely to have a predominant emotional state, some habitual thought patterns, strategies and habits. Do you want to make changes? Whether you are dealing with change in social systems, organizations or your own life, ask these questions:

■ What keeps the present situation in place?
■ What new arrangement do I want that will keep the benefits of the old, while losing its drawbacks?

If you want to change a habit, you have to look at what keeps it in place and what it is doing for you. The strength of the habit is not in the habit itself, but in what it achieves for you. The balancing loops keep it in place for some purpose or purposes. You may know what they are, or you may not. So ask yourself:

■ What is this habit trying to accomplish that is important to me?
■ How important is this to me now?
■ How can I accomplish the same thing in another, better way?

These questions will destabilize the status quo. Then you need to create another attractor:

■ What do I want to do instead?
■ Can I replace this habit with something new that will keep all the benefits of the old habit?

By levelling the old attractor and creating a new one, you can bring yourself to that crucial in-between point when it will be easy to fall into the new attractor.

Here is an example from a friend of ours. He had a habit of biting his nails. When he asked himself what kept the habit in place, he guessed it was work-related stress. His colleagues were not pulling their weight and he was left to do a lot of work that was not rightly his. This made him angry, but he never expressed it directly. Simple inattention also held the habit in place; he was unaware of his body and how he felt when he bit his nails. The initial problem was nail biting, but it led to many insights. Asking the systems question of what kept the habit in place led to deeper insights than asking, 'How can I stop this habit?' He made a number of changes to create a better attractor state. He bought some worry beads, and learned to be more aware of his feelings and his physical body. He started to be more assertive at work and refused to cover for others to the extent he had previously. This all took time, but now he is acting very differently *and* not biting his nails. This is also a good example of how our habits and actions work together as a system. They all connect. To stop a small action like biting his nails, our friend had to make some fundamental changes in how he thought and acted in relation to others.

---

1 Richmond, B., 'Systems thinking: critical thinking skills for the 1990s and beyond', *System Dynamics Review*, 9, 2, pp.113–33

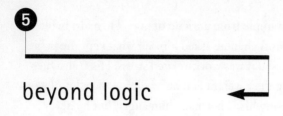

beyond logic

Logic, n. Source of reasoning, proof, thinking or inference.
The Concise Oxford Dictionary, fifth edition

Logic is held to be clear, effective thinking, the best way to solve problems. This seems strange. We do not naturally think in a very logical way and our most creative thought is in leaps of imagination that are painstakingly filled in later with logical steps to justify them. Our thinking is naturally emotional and associative, and sometimes we undervalue this aspect and over-value logic. In this chapter we want to go beyond logic...

Logic has its place, but it is inadequate to deal with a world of complex systems. The world is not logical, it is messy, incomplete and usually ambiguous. A whole new discipline of 'fuzzy logic' has developed[1] because judgements and decisions are rarely clear cut, they are approximate and uncertain. Logical language tends to deal in 'yes' or 'no', fuzzy logic in 'maybe' and 'perhaps'. Fuzzy logic may be more applicable to complex systems. Traditional logic is linear: A follows B follows C, marching towards a conclusion. Systems are non-linear, in other words the whole is qualitatively different and greater than the sum of its parts.

Systems create some strange and illogical paradoxes. Take the problem of traffic congestion. Too many cars on the road create traffic jams and slow, congested road networks. The obvious and logical answer is to add roads – more road space would surely thin the traffic. Not necessarily. Adding routes to an already congested network will only slow it down. This is known as the Bräss paradox, formulated by the German researcher Dietrich Bräss in 1968. It developed from the experience of the city planners in Stuttgart in the late 1960s, who tried to ease town centre traffic congestion by adding a street. When they did so, the traffic got worse. It was not the roads that were the problem, but the junctions – the *connections* between the roads, just what you would expect as systems thinkers. More roads give more junctions and so more possible congestion points. When the Stuttgart council blocked off the new road, the flow improved. We think all transport ministers ought to have the Bräss paradox in big letters framed on their wall. It might help them avoid some costly mistakes. It also has implications for designing the best way for information to flow in business and for communication between team members. There is an optimum number of routes and journeys in the flow of traffic or information; more is not necessarily better.

Thinking in systems terms, adding new roads to a congested network can create a second problem perfectly exemplified by the London orbital motorway, the infamous M25. Finished in 1982, the M25 was built to ease congestion by siphoning traffic away from London and providing a route around the capital rather than through it. It worked well – far too well. Not only did it take traffic from London, but it created traffic – it made journeys so easy that people and firms used it in preference to other forms of transport. The road was soon carrying more traffic than it was built to cope with. The consequences were predictable – bad congestion and increasing maintenance costs. The more use a road gets, the more wear and tear on its fabric, and the more roadworks needed

beyond logic

to repair it. The more roadworks, the more congestion.
A reinforcing loop has built up.

Plans are in progress to add more lanes to the M25. This
looks suspiciously like doing more of the same, trying to solve a
problem with the same thinking that created it. Eventually, a balancing loop will set in. The road will become so congested and
unpleasant that people will avoid it and use other forms of transport, thus easing congestion and decreasing the maintenance.
A reasonable balance point will be reached, regardless of the
number of lanes. Adding lanes pushes the problem into the future
and makes it worse (more lanes, more maintenance costs). We
hope the M25 planners will stop before the surrounding areas
come to resemble Los Angeles on a bad day.

The M25 is an example of a basic systems pattern known as
the tragedy of the commons. When there is an attractive common
resource more and more people tend to use it. The more people
use it, the less attractive it becomes, until it loses its value to
everyone. Every individual user acts in their own best interest,
but the result is a loss for everybody. More on this later.

Systems thinking takes in logic, but also goes beyond it, adding
two crucial dimensions that logic lacks.

One is time.

The other is self-reference and recursion.

Taking Time

Logic does not take account of time. It is timeless and based on *if–then* statements that translate as cause and effect. For example, water boils at 100° Centigrade, therefore, *if* the temperature rises to 100°C, *then* the water boils. Therefore, 100°C causes the water to boil. (Everything else being equal, of course.) Time is not taken into account.

Now let's see what happens when we try to map this reasoning onto a system, for example how we maintain a constant body temperature. *If* your body temperature rises, *then* you sweat. However, *if* you sweat, *then* your body temperature will fall. So the logical conclusion is, if your temperature rises, then your temperature falls. This is a logical nonsense that we nevertheless experience every day.

This shows how logic is not the same as cause and effect, because cause and effect take place in time. Although logic can often be reversed, cause and effect cannot. Systems operate with feedback circles of cause and effect, as already mentioned, so an 'effect' in any part of the circle can be seen as a 'cause' for a change in another element in the circle *at a later time*.

Here is another puzzle. You will need to think about time to solve it. (Hint.) A man lives by a railway track and likes to stroll across the bridge and watch the trains every day. The line carries both passenger trains and freight trains. The man never stays more than a few minutes on the

bridge and he makes a note afterwards of whether he sees
a passenger train or a freight train. Over the course of a year,
he notices that 90 per cent of the trains he sees have been
freight trains. A logical conclusion would be that as he sees
more freight than passenger trains, there really are more.
However, when he grumbles about the lack of passenger
trains to the station staff, he is surprised to learn that exactly
the same number of passenger trains and freight trains go
through the station every day. If the man makes random
trips to the bridge to watch the trains, how does he manage
to see such a disproportionate number of freight trains?
(Answer on page 113.)

Self-Reference and Recursion

It always takes longer than you think, even when you take this
into account.

Hofstadter's Law

What are self-reference and recursion? Self-reference means
a distinction is applied to itself, for example, 'There is no need to
be confused by your confusion!' This may jolt you out of a stuck
state, because it lifts you out of confusion into thinking about
how you can deal with confusion – which is a shift to a higher
level. Politicians use self-reference of another kind to dodge
embarrassing questions by pointing the finger at their accusers.

Recursion is applying self-reference like a spiral staircase
to bring you to higher and higher levels. You continually circle

back to the same point, but at a higher level. Recursions can be endless, like looking at yourself in a mirror looking at yourself...

Complex systems usually contain both self-reference and recursion as part of the structure of their feedback loops. Systems involving human communication always do.

Perhaps the best way to show self-reference is with another puzzle:

There is three misstakes in this sentence.
Can you find them?

First there is a grammatical mistake – it should read, 'There *are* three mistakes.' Second, 'mistakes' is misspelt. You could look forever for the third mistake *inside* the sentence; the third mistake is that there are only two mistakes in the sentence. You have to take a jump outside the sentence to see it. Self-reference confounds logic, for if there are three mistakes, then the sentence is correct, but if the sentence is correct then the sentence must be wrong. And so on.

What of the Cretan who, in Epimedes' famous paradox, says, 'All Cretans lie'? This is a self-referential message, it folds in on itself. As an observer of Cretans placing himself outside the group, he tells the truth to reveal a lie. As an observer of Cretans and including himself in that group, he lies in order to tell the truth. An observer may refer to their own observing in their observations. This plays havoc with linear logic.

Whenever there is self-reference, applying linear thinking within that frame of reference creates a paradox with no way out. The frame of reference is confused with the items in that frame. This might be simply an interesting philosophical point until you remember that human communication is full of these mixed messages. The messages given by social position, power structure, culture and mood may all clash with the bare words spoken. Language is never simply information. For example, we have all met the person who says, 'Yes,' when their body language is screaming, *'No!'* And what passes for good-natured banter between friends would be unacceptable in a work context. Often this is clear, and we all have skill and experience in separating these levels, although they may be very confusing. Have you ever been praised for a piece of work in a slightly sneering voice? It is hard to know what message to act on.

The most psychotoxic communication of all is the double bind which gives two messages and then makes you wrong whichever you choose, while forcing you to make a choice. An example is telling someone to be more assertive and not do as others say. When they are assertive they are made wrong for obeying advice. When they are not assertive they are told to be assertive. If they question this logic, they can be trapped in the frame by a reply like, 'Now you are confused. Why don't you think for yourself?'

These are the sort of paradoxes in communication that can drive you crazy, unless you can take what is called a *metaposition*. *Meta* is a Greek word meaning 'above and beyond', so taking a metaposition is being able to jump outside the frame you have been boxed in and to comment on the relationship between the two messages. Do they clash? Do they complement each other? What does each mean? A metaposition is a systems view. In the last example a metaposition would be to show how the two messages of assertion and obedience clash *and refuse to accept a reply that puts the question back into the obedience/assertion box.*

So systems thinking keeps us out of these stuck situations. It is the difference between being inside the system where the feedback loops and vicious circles just take you back to your starting-point and being able to get outside to take an overview. We will look at this in more detail later.

Limiting Mental Models

Mental models come in two varieties – those that make life more difficult by leading to stuck situations and those that make life easier by solving problems. The question is, how can we have fewer of the first kind and more of the second? Here are some traps you can set to snare the thinking that creates stuck situations for yourself and others:

1. LIST THE DIFFICULTIES

The best way to flush out limiting mental models that are stopping you from solving a problem is to be very clear about what you want. Set your goal. Then ask the basic systems question:

'What stops me achieving this goal?'

What are the most important factors that seem to be stopping you from getting what you want in the situation?

Now, just for the sake of argument, assume these are difficulties created by how you are thinking about the problem rather than real constraints in the situation.

Ask of each difficulty, *'How is that a problem?'* and write down the answers.

Then ask, *'What would have to happen for that not to be a problem?'*

Look particularly carefully at any answers that assume a lack of skill or resources in yourself or others. These may be limiting mental models.

2. THE LEFT-HAND COLUMN

Another useful way of getting at mental models is the left-hand column technique, originally developed by Chris Argyris and Donald Schon,[2] and elaborated by Nick Ross and Art Kleiner.[3] This is a good technique when you have a difficult problem with another person in a business or personal relationship. You might like to try it now.

Remember a typical frustrating conversation you had with the person. Take a sheet of paper and on the right side, write down what you said. On the left side, write down what you were thinking to yourself, regardless of whether you said it or not.

Look dispassionately at your left-hand column and ask yourself some questions:

What kinds of beliefs would give rise to those thoughts?
What stopped you from saying them?
What does this tell you about your beliefs in this situation?

You are not trying to resolve the situation directly with this exercise, but becoming aware of the limiting beliefs that are holding a problem in place is sometimes enough to suggest a solution.

Here is a short example from training we conducted. A man called John was having trouble with a business colleague. They were both on the same team working on a project, but John thought his colleague was not pulling his weight. A typical conversation would go like this:

Left-Hand Column	Right-Hand Column
(WHAT JOHN THOUGHT)	**(WHAT WAS SAID)**
	John: Have you finished that report yet?
Oh, the same excuses. Why can't he get his work done on time?	Colleague: Not quite, it'll be ready in a couple of days.
	John: When can we expect it? We can't progress with the project without that report.
A couple of days! I'll believe that when I see it.	Colleague: Couple of days at most. I've been really busy this week. Sorry.
Here come the excuses.	Also, I was waiting for those figures you were going to send me.
	John: I sent them last week.
	Colleague: They weren't in the format I needed, so I had to convert them. It took a little time.
You never asked for any format. It wasn't my fault.	John: OK.

Looking at this dialogue further, John found that he really wasn't seeing himself as part of a team, but as someone who did particular tasks within it. He did not get a sense of team accomplishment. He also saw that he assumed it was his colleague's responsibility to ask for what he wanted and not for him to find out. Lastly he assumed that to try and discuss these issues would be futile, that his colleague would be upset and wouldn't be able to handle the issue, and that it was better left alone, even though the situation was annoying.

These sorts of issues can be frustrating, and part of the problem is that as frustration and anger build, it becomes more and more difficult to have a reasonable discussion. The way forward is not to say out loud what is in the left-hand column. That would be counter-productive and often hurtful. What is important is to honestly put forward your difficulty and ask about the problems the other person is experiencing and how the situation looks from their point of view.

In this case, when John did talk to his colleague, he found that he was taking on too much of the work of the team and this was why he was having trouble finishing the report on time. He was worried about this but did not know how to raise the issues without appearing incompetent. He was very proud to be on the team and the success of the project was very important to him. Other team members were letting this situation continue. It wasn't just one person's problem; in the end the whole team came together to sort out how work was allocated and to improve communications between them.

3. LISTEN TO THE LANGUAGE

Limiting mental models act like rules and they show up in certain key words and phrases. There are certain phrases that will immediately alert you. Listen for these in what you say, in what you write, in what others say and, particularly, in your own internal dialogue or self-talk.

First listen for judgements. Judgements are authoritative statements about second order reality, the world of meaning, not physical fact.

Everything that is said is said by someone. There is no such thing as a description of reality that is not *someone's* description. However, statements can become disembodied and masquerade as reality itself, rather than someone's opinion. Once you realize this, you can decide whether you want to act on this received knowledge. It may have worked in the past, but is it applicable now?

Useful generalizations can become set clichés and demand to be taken as true in every case. But very few judgements are true of every situation, because we are open systems and therefore a slightly different starting-point can give a totally different end result, needing a different solution.

Listen to yourself and others and question any judgements. Are they really applicable? Be particularly suspicious of any statement that is preceded by the word 'obviously':

'Obviously, we cannot take on more staff.'
'Surgery is the answer to this problem.'
'Things will get worse before they can get better.'
'No pain, no gain.'
'Sales are bound to be badly affected by the economic situation.'
'We cannot afford any more investment in that project.'
'I'm not good at relationships.'

There are three ways to question judgements:

'Who says?'
'So what?'
'Why not?'

The best way will depend on what context you are in. (We do not recommend the second choice with a superior in a work situation.)

'Ought', 'should', 'have to' and 'must' are words that show that a rule is operating, and that rule may be a limiting mental model.
   Some examples:

'You must cut spending on project A.'
'You should take this medicine.'
'You must wear these clothes.'
'You have to tell her.'

Question these by asking: *'What would happen if I did not?'*
   This is a useful question because it gets at the imagined consequences behind the rule. There may be a very good reason for the rule, but it is always worth asking, even if only silently, to yourself.
   Another way of dealing with any of these phrases is to change them to 'could' in your mind and feel the difference this makes.
   So, 'I must cut my spending' becomes 'I could cut my spending.' Now the coercion has gone and it becomes a choice rather than a chore.

Conversely, 'ought not', 'shouldn't' and 'mustn't' also show rules. When you hear these, turn the last question around and ask, *'What would happen if I did?'* to get at the imagined consequences.

Again, the rule may be realistic and sensible, and the consequences unwelcome, but it is worth checking.

'Cannot' is another word that may show a limiting mental model. When you hear this, ask the basic systems question, *'What stops me?'*

Types of words such as 'ought', 'should', 'mustn't' and 'can't' are known in linguistics as *modal operators*. We suggest you set up a mental trap to catch modal operators, because they set limits and often cloak limiting mental models.

Finally, and paradoxically, there are a whole class of words called *universals*, for example, 'all', 'every', 'never', 'always', no one' and 'everyone'. These are generalizations. They claim there are no exceptions – but there are *always* exceptions.

Some examples of universals:

'Everyone is doing it this way.'
'You should never say that.'
'We've always done it that way.'
'No one has ever objected.'

Universals are limiting because if you accept them at their face value they close down choice and the search for other possibilities. Whenever you hear these universals, ask whether there have ever been any exceptions.

Mental Models as a Leverage Point

A business is structured through the mental models of the people who operate it. First we have the ideas and then we create the reality. The structure of the system may cause problems, but solving any business problem will always involve questioning the mental models of the people who run the business. Often changing a mental model is the leverage point that leads to breakthrough.

Here is an example. An electrical engineering firm changed their system of order processing. Now it worked more smoothly and shortened the time (or so they thought), between the customer's order being received and delivered. However, they seemed to be getting more customer complaints about delivery time, not fewer. This was very worrying.

Normal orders were processed within two days of being received. Stocks were kept high so there were no bottlenecks that could cause a delay. The management could not understand what was happening and considered trying to improve the already effi-cient processing department. However, when they looked at their order processing department as a part of the total system, they dis-covered some interesting facts. When the orders came in, they had to be checked. Those that were correct were forwarded to the fac-tory to be filled. This part of the system worked smoothly and effi-ciently. Orders that were incomplete had to be followed up and this could take time. A significant proportion of incomplete orders turned out to be those that needed credit approval, but they did not show up as a delay because they were entered as 'orders processed' in the books, even though they were waiting on credit approval.

When management looked at these orders they found that the numbers of orders on credit hold was significant and this was affecting the overall delivery time. Looking further, they found that over 90 per cent of these orders on credit hold were eventually approved for credit, which suggested that the real bottleneck was nothing to do with what their people did – they were working as hard as they could – but was due to the rules that governed credit approval. These rules were too stringent. So the leverage point in the system was the company rules for approval of credit orders. By relaxing these rules they reduced the orders that were on credit hold, dramatically reduced the overall delay and still caught orders where credit was really problematical, so there was no increase in bad debts.

Here the leverage point was a belief about what constituted credit worthiness. Also, the bottleneck was hidden because the orders needing credit approval were counted as processed, so the second leverage point was to change the criteria for what counted as a processed order. What you measure in a system and how you measure it will limit what you see and therefore what you can do. When an element is not measured, it is invisible – but it still affects the system.

Unless solving a problem leads to a shift in mental models, it hasn't been completely solved. Do we learn from experience? Only if the experience leads us to re-evaluate our mental models. What sort of mental models do you want?

How to Have Rigid, Limiting Mental Models

1. Insist that your ideas are how reality 'really' is.
2. Have a narrow set of interests to ensure you delete a lot of experiences.
3. Do not tolerate ambiguity; jump to conclusions as fast as possible.

4 Whenever people and events do not behave as you expect, have a fund of creative explanations.

5 Use lots of modal operators ('must', 'mustn't', 'should', 'shouldn't', 'cannot') and never question them.

6 Use many universals ('all', 'every', 'nobody', 'never') and do not admit exceptions.

7 Be quick to generalize from one example.

8 Set up plenty of one-sided, unfocused experiences to provide evidence for your ideas.

9 Blame failures on individuals (don't forget yourself).

10 Think in straight lines of cause and effect.

11 Never be curious.

12 Never update your beliefs in the light of experience.

How to Have Systemic Mental Models

1 Admit your mental models are your best guess at the moment and be on the lookout for better ones.

2 Have wide interests.

3 Be comfortable with ambiguity.

4 Be curious about, and pay particular attention to, experiences that seem to contradict your mental models.

5 Have a wide time horizon to look for feedback.

6 When confronted with a problem, look at the assumptions you are making about the situation as well as the situation itself.

7 Look for relationships, how events fit together.

8 Look for loops and circles of cause and effect, the effect of one cause being the cause of another effect.

Answer to the Train Puzzle

The man sees only a small part of the system and projects his limited experience onto the whole system. If he sees nine times as many freight as passenger trains, then does this mean there are nine times as many? No. What stops him seeing all the passenger trains? It is the time element. Freight trains come six minutes after passenger trains. The odds of the man arriving after a passenger train and before a freight train are nine to one, because for 54 minutes in every hour, a freight train is the next to appear. Only for six minutes in every hour will a passenger train be expected. When you see the whole picture, the answer is obvious.

---

1 Kosco, B., *Fuzzy Logic*, Flamingo, 1993
2 Argyris, C., and Schon, D., *Theory in Practice*, Jossey-Bass, 1974
3 Ross, N., and Kleiner, A., 'The ladder of inference' in Peter Senge *et al.*, *The Fifth Discipline Fieldbook*, Doubleday, 1994, p.246

SUMMARY: PART TWO

Mental Models

■ Mental models are the ideas and beliefs we use to guide our actions. We use them to explain cause and effect, and to give meaning to our experience.

■ Our mental models themselves form a system.

■ We need to understand our own mental models because we use them to make sense of other systems.

■ Mental models are created and maintained in four ways:
Deletion – selecting and filtering experience, blocking out some parts.
Construction – creating something that is not there.
Distortion – twisting experience, reading different meanings into it.
Generalization – one experience comes to represent a whole class of experiences.

■ There are a number of factors that produce misleading feedback:
Regression. Extreme events are unrepresentative as a basis for prediction and misleading if a change towards the average is taken as evidence for the effectiveness of a course of action.
Time focus. Unfocused effects can occur anytime after their presumed cause. Focused effects are limited to a particular time horizon. Unfocused effects are not reliable evidence.
One-sided experiences are those where only one result is memorable, anything else being a non-event.

Two-sided experiences are those where any result is memorable. Two-sided, focused experiences provide the best feedback for mental models.

Cause and Effect

■ In systems, causes are relationships between influencing factors rather than single events.
■ Systems thinking disposes of three fallacies:

❶ Cause and effect are separate and the effect comes after the cause.
❷ Effect follows cause closely in time and space.
❸ The effect is proportional to the cause.

■ Closed systems are isolated from their environment.
■ Open systems are open to their environment.
■ Chaos theory deals with complex systems where a small change in the initial conditions can make a huge difference – complex systems are not predictable. However, there may be some simple rules at the heart of very complex systems.

■ To deal with complex systems:
Define the boundaries of the system.
Look for attractors (stable states where the system tends to settle).

■ To change a complex system:
Destabilize the old attractor state.
Create a new attractor state.

Beyond Logic

■ Logic alone is inadequate to deal with systems:
Cause–effect links in logic are timeless and in systems they
take place in time.
Logic cannot deal with self-reference, where a statement
refers to itself. To solve the paradoxes of self-reference,
you need a systems view, or metaposition, outside the frame
of reference.

■ You can catch limiting mental models by:
Listing the difficulties and asking if they exist outside or
within your thinking.
Making a 'left-hand column' of what you thought in a problem situation as well as what you said.
Listening for certain phrases: judgements, modal operators
and universals.

■ The best leverage points for change are often the mental
models that are supporting the structure of the system.

thinking in
new ways

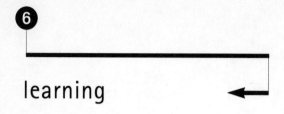

learning

We experience ourselves as the centre of our world. Our influence spreads like ripples in a pool. We do not know on what distant shore they will eventually come to rest. We do know the wave of feedback that comes back to us – although not always how we created it. Sometimes it is hard to believe it comes from us at all. The more we are aware of the effects of our actions and experience ourselves as active rather than passive, the more fulfilling life becomes. This is learning – changing ourselves using the feedback from our actions.

Learning may have unpleasant associations for you. But it does not only mean passively absorbing facts at school or coming to benefit from bad experiences. Learning is deeper than this and has very little to do with being formally taught by others, for we are always our own teacher. We can learn from everything we do.

Learning is creating results – the only way we have of changing ourselves and becoming more of who we want to be. Learning creates and recreates our mental models.

You can learn about life, or you can learn by living, and while the first type of learning may be useful, and help you with the second, it is the second that makes the most difference.

In this chapter we want to look at three related questions:

- How do we learn in and about complex systems?
- How can we learn more effectively?
- What stops us learning?

Learning as a System

Learning is a process – something you *do*. It means change. Your experience changes you.

How do you know when you have learned something? You know more about the world and other people. You are able to do something you could not do before. You may have a new skill. You may even rethink your beliefs and values as a result, and ultimately change the sort of person you are. Although learning sometimes seems to be a specialized activity that has to be supervised and take place in particular places, it really takes place all the time. You can learn from everything you do, because learning is one of the most basic feedback loops in living. And you learn best in your own way – by reading, listening talking and doing. Learning at its simplest is a basic feedback loop.

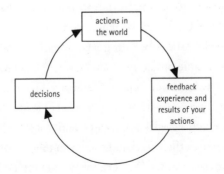

Basic learning feedback loop

You take action, you experience the results of those actions and you take decisions based on those results, which lead to more actions. It is a reinforcing feedback loop: more actions lead to more feedback lead to more decisions. This loop is very simplified, because as it stands, the decisions are random, they have no purpose. We actually base our decisions on whether we get what we want. Someone is missing from the picture above – you. So we need to redraw...

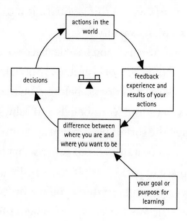

Learning loop

This is a balancing loop. You learn for a purpose, there is a gap between where you are and where you want to be, and you take action to close the gap. Your goal may be to know more, to influence a colleague or family member, or to achieve a business objective. It may be to get some academic qualifications, as a passport to the job you want. It may be simply for fun! Enjoying yourself is as much a goal as anything else (it may be the most sought after goal in the world, judging from the size of the industries there are to satisfy it). We certainly learn better when we enjoy the experience as well as gaining something from it.

So, your actions gets results – you may or may not be closer to your goal. These results are your feedback. Now what?

Your next action may not take the feedback into account, so you repeat the same experience. This is the realm of habits and scripts. These are useful in many situations – we automate many of the straightforward parts of our lives, so we can learn and think about the more important aspects. Even here, however, we pay attention to the feedback that tells us whether these habits are effective at doing what we want them to do. Sometimes habit invades parts of our lives where it does not belong, for example the salesperson who uses the same script on every customer, regardless of the circumstances, or the manager who treats all their staff the same. Fixed actions get varied results. They do not close the gap between what you want and what you have got. If the salesperson or manager wants to be the best they can, they must keep their goals in mind and vary what they do.

So learning is taking decisions and changing what we do in response to the feedback we get. We are not isolated, so what we do changes the world as well. In the next trip round the feedback loop, we are a slightly different person in a slightly different world. We have to keep changing in order to survive, because the world does not stand still, it is constantly moving, and in order to keep your balance, and even stay where you are, you have to shift your weight all the time. It is like standing in water, with eddies and currents pushing and jostling around you. You will overbalance if you try to stand rigidly. To stay upright and balanced, you have to move and shift your weight the whole time. This is *dynamic equilibrium*. We cannot stand still even if we want to.

Most of the time we act on feedback. We see whether our decisions and actions have taken us any nearer our goal. If not, we do something else. If so, we do the same again. This all happens in an instant; it takes far longer to describe than do.

This learning cycle is called simple learning, single loop learning, or sometimes first order learning[1] or adaptive learning.[2] Simple learning leaves your mental models intact. You select your actions and make your decisions from a fixed set of choices that are part of your mental models. This does not alter your world view. Most of our learning is simple learning.

There are two sorts of single loop learning. One happens *in time* and the other happens *through time*. The first, learning in time, uses feedback in the moment. For example, earlier we asked you to touch a full stop on the page with the tip of your finger. When you did so, you had to move the tip of your finger, based on how you saw the alignment and whether you were on target. It all happened in an instant. If we asked you to do the same thing with the full stop at the end of this sentence, the same thing would happen. Your physical co-ordination lets you do both, you do not have to remember what happened last time in order to do it again. This is true for most simple tasks and how well you perform depends on the quality of your attention at the time. You use the feedback *in that moment*.

In more complex skills you need feedback through time. You learn by repetition. For example, suppose you are learning to play tennis. You play a shot in the moment. It goes wide. That was not what you wanted. So the next time you make slight adjustments based on what you learned from the previous shot. You find out what it feels like to over hit and under hit and time it just right. You change yourself to acquire the skill. We might argue that the whole intent of feedback *through* time is so you can operate more effectively with feedback *in* time. Your hand-eye co-ordination has been built up from childhood, so you can easily touch the full stop without practice. In the tennis example, the novice is the one who is starting to build their skills with feedback through time. The expert makes the stroke from feedback in time, that is the result of much practice.

When you are arguing with someone else, trying to influence them, not only will you be paying attention to their voice, words and body language in the moment, but also using what you know about them, and what you know of influencing and communication skills. As you learn from your experience, you become a better communicator. In this type of learning, you use the feedback to do better *next time*. So there are feedback loops not only within an action, but also in a series of actions over time. It is this type of learning that changes us.

Single loop learning is a balancing feedback loop and tends towards adaptation and stability. In organizations it tends towards procedures, institutions, 'the system' of doing things. After a while these practices may become stuck and hinder new ideas. Nothing inhibits future success like making procedures to formalize what generated a previous success. An organization selects people who think in the same way it operates, so they are likely to continue on the same path – another balancing loop that works against change when it is needed. Individuals and organizations may become increasingly inward-looking, more and more a closed system. Closed systems decay and run down. What began as a break-through and a success becomes the norm, then unquestioned. For change and renewal a new type of learning is needed.

Generative Learning

There is a second type of learning where our mental models are brought into the feedback loop. This is called generative learning, or double loop learning.[3]

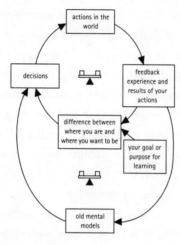

Generative learning

In generative learning we allow our mental models to be influenced, perhaps changed, by the feedback. The extra loop may be a reinforcing one if it strengthens our old mental models and so leads to the same decisions, or it may be a balancing one if it makes us question them. This loop will only be a balancing loop if we have a certain goal – to be curious, to continuously improve and question our ideas and beliefs. Without this goal, the loop will be a reinforcing one – unless the feedback is so bizarre as to shake us out of our complacency.

Generative learning is the balancing loop, the way we update our mental models. It gives us a wider number of choices, new strategies and decision rules to apply. The same feedback taken through different mental models will lead to different decisions and so different action.

No Learning

Repeat the same action regardless of the result, paying no attention to feedback.

Examples: Habits, using scripts regardless of result.

Simple Learning

Pay attention to feedback and change your action depending on the results you get. Your choices and actions are dictated by your mental models, which are not changed.

Examples: Trial and error, rote learning, learning a skill.

Generative Learning

Allow feedback to affect and change your mental models of the situation. This leads to new strategies and new classes of action and experience that were not possible before.

Examples: Learning to learn, questioning your assumptions, seeing a situation in a different way.

learning

Generative learning leads to new choices. We may see the whole situation differently. We may question fundamental assumptions, even the sort of person we are. Generative learning in business leads to questions about what sort of business it is and what else it could be. The basic questions that drive generative learning are:

- 'What are my assumptions about this?'
- 'How else could I think about this?'
- 'What else could this mean?'
- 'How else could this be used?'

One example of generative learning on a large scale is the way the Internet has changed. It started modestly enough in America in the early 1970s connecting ARPAnet, an experimental computer network, with other radio and satellite networks. ARPAnet was a military support network involved in researching how to build communications that would survive damage such as nuclear or conventional bomb attacks. As a result of its military origins, the Internet is a highly flexible, damage-resistant communications network because the computers and not the network are responsible for establishing communication. One computer can talk to another by routing through any computer on the network. This is like being able to make a telephone call by connecting through any other telephones and so through to another exchange if your own exchange is out of action.

More and more university computer systems joined the network, and the embryonic Internet coalesced mainly as a means for academic research. At the start, universities joined because of the research possibilities; it was a way to share information quickly and easily. However, as it developed, the Internet did not simply become a better and faster military or academic research network, but broadened to become a network of networks, a universal communications, advertising and publishing medium. Perhaps eventually it will form a universal library, where the library ticket is a computer, a modem and an Internet account. All this has happened because people saw possibilities beyond the use at the time.

Simple learning in business will improve a company. It will do what it has always done more efficiently or more quickly in a particular area. Generative learning in business will change the way the business operates and perhaps open up new areas entirely. For example, large supermarket chains are no longer just a convenient place to buy your food cheaply. You can buy clothes, gifts, videos, toys and books from them, and now they are issuing cash cards and behaving like banks.

More and more firms are finding that with intense competition for the actual product, it is customer service and customer loyalty that make the difference, and after-sales service has become like a product that is sold together with the main product. Sometimes the quality of the after-sales service determines whether the customer buys the main product at all.

Entrenched mental models are what keeps a company from improving and solving problems. These mental models are themselves the result of ineffective learning. For example, for one company, falling sales are a signal to redouble the sales efforts – they may try a marketing drive, increased advertising, more training for the sales teams, higher targets and bigger bonuses for achieving them. This may not work as it did in the past. From a systems point of view, the higher sales targets may well encourage the sales force to promise more special orders and quicker delivery. But the pressure of meeting these extra demands may result in *slower* delivery times. Then customers complain and drift away, leading to greater sales efforts... The mental model of trying to replace lost sales with new ones can lead to even worse trouble. Another model would be to think about redoubling efforts to keep existing customers and create a reinforcing loop for a good reputation by word of mouth that would then attract other customers. There would be a time delay and the company would have to tolerate falling sales without seeing the results of their new strategy. This could be hard.

Mental models are often metaphors and hard to question because they are not directly expressed. For example, one that made sense for many years was the idea of organizing business like a pyramid, with a small number of decision-makers at the top broadening out with more followers on the base. Single loop learning would be trying to use the new communications technology to build a better pyramid. Small hope. In the present shifting, decentralized global markets, pyramids are organizational dinosaurs. They cannot respond fast enough. Many companies have down-sized and squashed corporate hierarchies into flat networks. And still there will come a time when flat networks will need to be adapted. These can rest on their laurels for a little while, but continual learning means not getting stuck in one model, but seeing how effective businesses can be built using hierarchies and networks, while staying open to other possibilities. No answer lasts forever. A management technique that cannot answer the problems it generates will become a passing fad, to be replaced by the next technique that addresses the problems generated by the last fad... The only way to stay ahead is to learn continuously.

You will have your own examples of generative learning in your life. We have a friend who used to worry about his health. He would take the slightest pain or ache, cough or cold as feedback that he was ill, and that meant a visit to the doctor. He believed that illness meant that there was something wrong with him which had to be fixed as soon as possible. He felt under siege from a hostile environment, full of lurking germs, waiting for him to lower his guard so they could attack. He thought he was lucky to be well at all. None of his illnesses were serious and his visits to the doctor, reading and personal development were all feedback that eventually shifted his self-image from a fundamentally ill person who happened to be well to a basically well person who became ill sometimes. He learned it was not unhealthy to be ill and this was a major change for him.

What Prevents Us Learning?

If learning is a system and we are getting feedback all the time, what stops us learning all the time?

DELETING PART OF THE FEEDBACK

We may not see the feedback because we concentrate on one part of the loop and ignore the other, like seeing only one side in a football match. Feedback forms a circle which can start anywhere and we decide where we start, which is cause and which is effect, based on our mental models.

For example, we are used to understanding the communication between teacher and learner as the teacher teaching the learner. Seen like this, it looks like a one-way, linear relationship, defined by role. But we could look at it another way. The teacher could not teach without feedback from the learner, as the teacher only knows what to do next by the learner's response. The learner's questions, answers, and expressions, both quizzical and satisfied, let the teacher know how to proceed. So the learner elicits from the teacher exactly what they need to learn. The better the learner does this, the more skilful the teacher appears. In that sense, the learner 'teaches' the teacher how to teach. And the teacher 'learns' how to teach from the interaction. This way of understanding is different from the normal, but just as valid. Here is the origin of the saying 'the best way to learn a subject is to teach it'. Both teacher and learner respond to feedback in the moment and this leads to a virtuous feedback loop.

However, there is another scenario. In this one, the learner does not ask questions and the teacher does not respond to that feedback (of not asking questions) by checking the learner's understanding of the lesson. What stops the teacher responding? Because they know they are a great teacher and the lack of questions just proves it! But the learner may not understand. If this happens in school, the result is often the classic complaint from the teacher, 'I taught them but they didn't learn' – a sentence that makes no sense. It is the educational equivalent of the medical joke 'The operation was a success but the patient died.'

To be successful, learner and teacher learn and teach together. It is a process that can be viewed from three different perspectives:

- The teacher's point of view.
- The learner's point of view.
- The relationship between the two.

The systems view is recursive, in other words it takes the distinctions (teaching and learning) and applies them again at a higher level to what is going on in the relationship. Now the person in the role of teacher can learn how to play that role even more skilfully. They may learn more about their subject from the learner's questions. They may learn how to be a good learner and how to be more flexible in presenting the material. The learner can understand their own learning process better and model their teacher, gaining an insight into the way of thinking that allows the teacher to know the material. In one sense, the role of teacher is a ghost role, for both sides are learning, although they are learning different things.

The human relationship between teacher and learner is crucial as well. We all have had the experience of learning from someone we like and respect. And of course the easiest way to learn a foreign language is to fall in love with a native speaker.

DYNAMIC COMPLEXITY

Human systems are very complex. We influence other people who influence many more in turn. Trying to track the ramifications is like trying to find your way through a particularly fiendish maze, where every move you make changes the whole maze. Just when you have worked out how to find the exit, your first step changes the maze completely.

Time delays are another factor. It is hard to connect cause and effect when they appear distant from each other in time and space. So we may blithely carry on producing industrial pollutants without knowing the long-term effects, while we reap the consequences of the generation before us. When we do not detect feedback it may be that the feedback has not worked its way round the system yet. As we have already seen, sometimes there are thresholds where nothing happens until a critical value is reached, then the whole system springs into life (or collapses). It is hard to find a balance where we do not react too early or too late unless you know the time delay.

Complex systems have some surprising properties that fly in the face of the linear sort of common sense we are used to. What seems the obvious answer may get us more deeply caught in the mire, or be exactly the wrong thing to do. The obvious way out in systems nearly always leads back in. This makes it harder to learn, because the feedback is puzzling. The solution may appear unbelievable, and even when we *know* it is the answer, a lot of courage and trust may be needed to actually do it.

For example, do you know what to do if your car goes into a skid? Joseph was driving some years ago in heavy rain and his car began sliding across the road out of control. He knew that he should turn into the skid, but in the split second of decision, he acted on a reflex and did what all his senses and a large rush of adrenaline told him to do – he tried to turn away from the skid to straighten the car. If you have ever been tempted to turn away from a skid, *don't* – it makes it worse, just as the theory says it will. Joseph's car finished its journey upside-down in the middle of the road facing in the opposite direction. Fortunately, no one else was involved and Joseph was lucky enough to escape with a cut arm.

MENTAL MODELS

Our mental models can stop us learning in a variety of ways. We tend to see what we expect and are mislead by the regression effect. We often see cause and effect as separate, and look for effects both proportional to and close to the cause in time and space. We try to use logic when human communication is full of self-reference and judge often by expectation rather than observation. We also attribute behaviour, success and failure to individuals, instead of to the structure and limits of the system. We judge how effective and successful we are too soon, before the feedback has worked its way round the system. Thus we do not appreciate the consequences of our actions.

MEASURING FEEDBACK

In order to learn, you have to act on your feedback. But you can only do this if you detect it. So your sensitivity to feedback has to match the range of feedback you are getting.

The way we perceive feedback is through our senses and they are very keen. We can see the light of a candle 10 miles away and our range of hearing spans 10 octaves – 16,000–20,000 cycles per second. We sense the feedback from our bodies, giving us a measure of our health and well-being. The more sensitive we are to the messages of our body, the better we can take care of our physical health and separate what needs attention from what will go away by itself. Pain, although unwelcome, is very useful feedback. It is a warning that something is wrong and needs attention. Without it, we would not know we were hurt or ill. Then we would not do anything about it and the consequences could be serious. Our senses also measure the feedback from our communication – the other person's changes in voice tone, the nuances of their body language.

From a systems point of view, the senses are only way we can receive feedback, so the more acute they are the better. Also, the more acute they are, the more pleasure we derive from them.

The limits of our sensitivity to feedback are often set by our mental models, our beliefs about what is possible or what we expect. The feedback is there, but we set our sights (and hearing and feeling) too low. This is true for our senses as well as the instruments we construct – we make instruments to detect what we expect will be there. For example, it has been known since 1974 that CFCs (chlorofluorocarbons) destroy atmospheric ozone.[4] In 1985 evidence of a deep hole in the ozone over the Antarctic was published.[5] This caused concern and surprise at NASA, because the satellite Nimbus 7 had been taking routine measurements of atmospheric ozone since 1978 and had never shown a dangerously low reading. The scientists at NASA checked their results and found that they had set their computers to reject very low ozone readings because they assumed that such readings would be due to an error in the instruments. NASA took the original data and ran the tests again without the computer bias, confirming that the ozone concentration had been falling steadily for seven years. So the mental models of the scientists had led them to design a highly sophisticated measuring system that was actually useless because it could not detect measurements that would disprove their models. On the individual level, this is much the same as claiming that people do not get hurt by your forthright remarks because they do not break down in tears.

PRECISION AND ACCURACY

Measurement brings us to the difference between precision and accuracy. Precision is how closely you can measure a value, for example 1.11407 is a more precise measurement than 1.0. It has more distinctions. However, if the answer you want is 2.0, then any other answer, however precise, would be inaccurate, in other words, wrong. Computers can measure things extremely precisely, to many decimal places, but they can still be inaccurate (to the same number of decimal places), if they are given the wrong data, or if we limit their range of measurement, as in the NASA example.

Precision is a measure of quantity, of number. Many things are easily measured in numbers, money for example, and quantity may be useful feedback. However, the most important things cannot be measured with numbers, such as perseverance, honesty, integrity, creativity and intelligence. These are just as much feedback as money and as important, if not more so. We measure them when for example we decide one person is more honest than another.

Even when we make accurate observations, see every nuance of another person's face and body language, and hear every variation in their voice tone, we still may not know the meaning. Being able to interpret body language comes from learning over time. This comes first by being sensitive to your own thoughts, feelings, voice and body language and linking them to your own internal state. Then when you hear a similar voice tone, you can empathize with the speaker's feelings because you are able to make the leap of imagination into their shoes. Sensitivity to others begins with sensitivity to yourself. Secondly, you learn by paying attention over time to confirm your intuitions. What looks like boredom may be thoughtfulness. Different people have different ways of demonstrating the same feeling.

WHEN DO WE ACT?

What is your feedback telling you? Do you have feedback loops that give you an adequate warning of problems? Or do they only tell you when the problem is upon you? Where do you set your thresholds? If you set them too low then you may react too soon. This is like waking up to every small noise during the night, including the natural ones of the house creaking or cars going past the window. Jealousy is another example – a jealous person is sensitive to the slightest signal that might just mean their partner is interested in another person. Hypochondria is another – taking every small ache or pain to the doctor. The same low threshold shows when we micromanage, trying to control every aspect of a job, or overteach, jumping in at the slightest mistake and not letting the learner manage their own learning. Another example is the person who is so anxious to avoid any confrontation that they will back down from their opinion at the slightest sign that you disagree with them. They want to be friendly, but we need friends who are different, who stimulate us, not boring one-dimensional doormats. Someone who always agrees often ends up isolated because they are not offering anything of themselves but only reflecting others.

Prevention is usually better than cure, but too low a threshold makes for a very rigid system. You need some freedom and room to manoeuvre. Crime prevention is one example where there has to be a balance. Ian's house was broken into a few years ago and money was stolen. Not wanting a repeat performance, he talked to the local crime prevention officer about how to make the house more secure. He could have put steel shutters on all the windows and reinforced bolts on all the doors, but that would have been extremely expensive. It would also have left him a prisoner in his own house. The hardest buildings to get in are also the hardest to get out of – prisons.

And total security is impossible. The best answer is a balance between cost, effectiveness, convenience and deterrent value. Ian put in a good burglar alarm system and increased the security on all the doors and windows.

The same balance applies to crime in general. A society that set out to prevent crime, setting its threshold really low, would have a huge, heavily armed police force, constant surveillance, telephone tapping and unlimited government powers to hold citizens and investigate their finances, politics and lifestyle. The price in civil liberties would be unacceptably high.

On the other hand, too high a threshold means that the system may only respond when the problem has reached a critical stage and it is hard to do anything. You do not wait until you need an ambulance before getting medical attention and you do not want to wait before the company is collapsing before intervening in how the business is run. Some people, of course, do wait until their relationships are on the critical list before paying attention.

The same applies to political and economic systems. A country does not wait until it is attacked before mobilizing its army, and politicians carefully follow economic indicators to try to keep the economy on track. Even so, they seem to make adjustments in the present on information that is months old. It is like driving while looking out of the rear-view mirror. We particularly need early warning feedback systems for our environment. The larger and more complex the system, the more it affects every part of our lives and the more potential for disaster if anything goes badly wrong. Equally, the more potential for health and well-being when things go right!

We have to find our own balance. We do not want to be so rigid as to never plant any water-lilies because eventually they will grow and cover the whole pond, but, having planted them, we would not want to wait until the last possible day before cutting them back!

QUESTIONS

Your senses give you immediate feedback. The other way to get feedback is by questions. Good questions get good feedback. The more precise and focused the question, the more useful the answer. So cultivate the art of asking good questions. Here are some from the previous section that you might find useful:

- Is the action you propose based on habit or feedback?
- What are your results so far?
- Do you have accurate feedback about the consequences of your previous actions?
- Do you know what effect you have been having?
- How might you find out?
- What are you assuming about the problem and the people involved?
- Where do you set your thresholds – how much are you willing to tolerate before acting?
  - in your health and well-being?
  - in your relationships?
  - in your profession?

1 Bateson, Gregory, *Steps to an Ecology of Mind*, Jason Aronson, 1987
2 Senge, Peter, *The Fifth Discipline*, Doubleday, 1990
3 Argyris, C., Putnam, R., and Smith, D., *Action Science*, Jossey-Bass, 1985
4 Molina, M., and Rowland, F., 'Stratospheric sink for chlorofluoromethanes: chlorine atomic catalyzed destruction of ozone', *Nature* 249 (1974), 810
5 Farman, J., Gardiner, B., and Shanklin, J., 'Large losses of total ozone in Antarctica reveal seasonal ClO/NO_2 interaction', *Nature* 315 (1985), 207

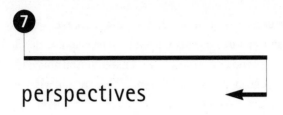

perspectives

A perspective is a point of view; unfamiliar points of view give very different interpretations. Many years ago a newspaper ran a weekly competition where you had to identify an everyday object from an extremely close up photograph. Very difficult. Try an experiment now. Look at the back of your hand. Now imagine zooming closer and closer until you are really close and all you can see is the pores of your skin. Would you recognize your hand? Now imagine pulling away until you can see your hand again. You can only recognize it when you are a certain distance away. When you are very close, its wholeness, its *handness*, just disappears. Emergence is one result of perspective. In the same way, sometimes we get so close to our experience it becomes confusing. We do not see the pattern. Understanding and recognition come with perspective.

Different perspectives can give surprisingly different views, even of something we know very well. Have you ever heard your own voice on tape? That is how others hear you, but you hear your voice differently – as it resonates in the bones of the head. The voice from the tape recorder is not your voice as you know it. You may have got used to photographs of yourself, but have you ever seen yourself on videotape? Now, thanks to video technology, we do have the gift to see ourselves as others see us, and most people have very mixed feelings.

World-wide, our view of ourselves changed forever when we saw the first pictures of Earth taken from space. For the first time we could see the Earth as a whole. That unmistakable globe of luminous green and blue is our home, the only one we have. On detailed pictures, you can see our impact on the planet – the patches of pollution around the major cities...

LATERAL, HORIZONTAL, VERTICAL AND MULTI-DIMENSIONAL THINKING

What we allow ourselves to see makes up our mental models and our mental models can limit our viewpoints, and the limited viewpoints reinforce our mental models – a reinforcing feedback loop. We see what we expect to see. And the same ways of looking lead to the same ways of thinking. This narrows our world.

Systems thinking is a different perspective. It looks at how experiences relate, how they go together to form greater wholes. At the same time a fundamental principle of systems thinking is to take as many different perspectives as possible. This is especially rewarding because the world is always richer than any representation we have of it, so the more perspectives, the richer the world appears.

Different perspectives will widen our mental models and wider mental models will lead to a further opening out of perspectives and set up a reinforcing loop that widens our world.

What stops us routinely enjoying different perspectives and learning from them? First, when we set too high a threshold for failure. Failure is unwelcome feedback. Some people can tolerate a great deal of failure (in other words, have a high threshold), before they start to question the assumptions they are operating under (i.e. their mental models).

The second is a mental model – that the meaning of what we do is in our intentions. This leads to doing the same actions and justifying an unwelcome result by saying you didn't mean it to turn out that way.

Thirdly, and most important, is a lack of curiosity. Curiosity is a state that goes beyond mental models – it questions them. When you are curious, driven to find out why and how something works (or does not work), then your mental models will be more flexible, more responsive to feedback.

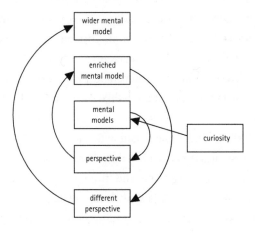

Widening perspectives

Curiosity generates perspectives. There are no wrong perspectives, only those that are useful and those that are not. And usefulness is a personal value judgement based on prior learning. So it is worth being curious about what could be useful to generate new viewpoints. Creativity and different sorts of intelligence all involve taking different viewpoints, and therefore getting different sorts of feedback.

Systems thinking is seeing situations and experience as a whole. You will not see them as a whole unless you either take a longer view, a step back to see the pattern, or you build up that whole from many different angles. Then you establish a different relationship to the situation and the different relationship can give a whole new appreciation, just as two eyes give binocular vision.

For example, a manager of a company that leased office equipment had one outstanding service engineer. Customers' photocopiers went wrong fairly regularly and it was often very difficult to discover the exact fault. Typically, the problem was intermittent and the machine would work fine as long as the engineer was there. Later, the problem would return.

The service department had compiled a bulky manual containing a series of exhaustive procedures designed to track down the cause of the problem when the engineer was not able to duplicate the fault on site. However, one engineer was exceptionally good at finding the faults without the help of the manual. The secret was simple. The engineer would call on the customer in the afternoon and before looking at the machine would sort through the discarded copies basket. Invariably, there would be some excellent examples of what was wrong and the engineer was nearly always able to locate and fix the fault without the help of the manual.

What was different? The engineer was broadening the time scale and searching the past for clues rather than the present, as well as seeing that what was useless in normal circumstances (wrong copies) was valuable information in the special repair circumstances.

Inside Out or Outside In

There are two crucially different and basic perspectives, sometimes called *objective* and *subjective*. Objective means looking from the outside in and, interestingly enough, has come to be equated with 'truthful'. Subjective means looking from the inside out and is usually considered less reliable. ('That's just your subjective view' usually means it doesn't count.) Think about these two perspectives without value judgements, in system terms.

An objective view is looking at a system from outside it.

A subjective view is looking at a system from inside it.

Systems thinking uses both views.

THE OBJECTIVE VIEW

In the final analysis, there can never be final objectivity, because you can never stand outside the system of which you are a part because then you would not exist. Total objectivity is meaningless because there is no observer to describe it. So whether you are being subjective or objective depends on how *you define the boundary* of the system you are considering.

Science tries to take as objective a view as possible, but even science must have an observer and we are finding in the strange contradictions of quantum physics that the observer cannot be left out of the equation. The observer influences the experiment.

Science does not actually prove anything, it makes hypotheses and tests them. Scientific knowledge is a series of constantly updated working hypotheses about the world. Science is tremendously valuable and has given us knowledge, understanding and quality of life, but it gives results that lead to a particular sort of understanding. There are many things we take for granted that cannot be proved in a scientific experiment for one of two reasons. Either they are not falsifiable (e.g. religious beliefs), or they cannot be isolated sufficiently from the system in which they are embedded to control all the variables, and therefore cannot be studied under 'scientific' conditions. Complex systems, like human relationships, have a dynamic complexity that science cannot unravel.

For example, neuroscience can give an excellent description of the brain, how the neurons work and what biochemical changes take place, right down to the molecular formula for the neuro-transmitters that are coursing in your brain and body right now, enabling you to see and hear, to understand and think about this book. However, it can tell you nothing of the richness of your experience, what it is like to be *you*, the personal meaning you make of these words, nor does it claim to. While it can give you the chemical composition of the scent of a rose, it can't tell you what it is like to smell one. Your experience is not reducible to the sparking between synapses or the ebb and flow of neurotransmitters. They are part of a smaller system in your body. Your experience is an emergent from the total system and one that you experience from the inside. You make meaning of it, you interpret it in terms of your model of the world. Change the neurotransmitters and the experience would be different, but one cannot be reduced to the other. Your brain may look like a lump of old porridge, but your mind does not look like that at all. To know your mind, we have to talk to you.

The same distinction applies at the collective level. We can measure and evaluate the art and ethos of our times, the sociological trends, the political movements, but culture is something we are inside, we experience it subjectively.

Science tends to be analytical, breaking things into smaller parts in order to understand them. Systems thinking builds up from elements to larger wholes.

Systems thinking takes both the subjective and the objective perspectives. It is very important you know which perspective you are taking at any time. Both are necessary. What is important is where you draw the boundary of the system – what distinctions you make, never forgetting you can never completely step outside the system of which you are a part. When you draw the systems boundary too narrowly, you make the mistake of reducing experience to a series of sparking neurons and flowing neurotransmitters. When you draw it too widely, you risk ignoring their very real effects.

THE SUBJECTIVE VIEW

Looking from the inside out, or taking the subjective view, our experience has a truth and directness to it. While individual experience may be misleading (is that a ghost or a shadow, a UFO or the sun reflecting off the clouds?), we validate our experience through shared understanding with others. We do not look to science to prove or disprove it for us. We don't seek objectivity.

There is a useful further division of this subjective perspective:

- Your own perspective from the inside out. *What the world looks like to you through your own filters, interests, mind and body. Take a moment to think deeply about something that is important to you. This is your viewpoint, it is your experience, not just an idea but a living, breathing reality.*
- Someone else's perspective. *This is a leap of the imagination, an attempt to get a flavour of another person's thinking and feeling 'as if' you were them. It is not your interpretation or judgement of what they are feeling, but an honest attempt to 'walk in their shoes'. This is a second subjective perspective.*

Taking someone else's perspective, sometimes known as second position, is essential. Whatever you do affects others and you need to know how they see it from their world.

One business we know used to hold meetings that continually

ended in deadlock – the sales manager would argue his position, the marketing senior manager would argue her position and the customer service manager would disagree with both of them. All the people were sincere and passionate about their beliefs. They regularly reached sincere and passionate stalemate.

We proposed they changed the format of their meetings. First the sales manager would make his presentation. Then both the marketing manager and customer service manager had to summarize it in a way that was completely acceptable to the sales manager. After a short pause, the marketing manager would make her presentation and the others had to put her case in a way that she completely accepted. Finally, the customer service manager would put his case and the others had to present it back to him in a way that was acceptable to him. Then the meeting proceeded, but now, because they had a sense of how the others felt, it was much more productive. We have also used a variation of this where one manager briefs another, who then has to sincerely present the first manager's case to the rest of the meeting. These methods are variations of getting the people concerned to understand not just intellectually , but also to experience the other person's point of view.

To understand any human system, you need to weave your perspective and other people's perspectives together. You may be part of the system you are trying to understand, in which case your perspective is as valuable and necessary as the others'. Your system may be a management meeting, a family dispute or a local political issue – something that matters to you and that you feel strongly about. Even if you are called in as an 'outside' consultant to look at a business, or as a counsellor to look at a family, you become part of that system by virtue of your involvement in it and the mental models you bring with you. The mental models of the other people are of course also part of the system.

In understanding human systems (businesses, families, relation-ships), be aware of your own thoughts and feelings, and also the thoughts and feelings of the other people involved – from their perspective. You do not have to agree with them, but unless you understand them, you will not understand the system.

Without both these two subjective perspectives, there is a danger of taking an analytical objective view of a system, trying to understand it by breaking it into smaller parts, and treating people as objects.

Once these different perspectives have given you a better under-standing of the system from the inside, you can take an objective view – a mental step outside – and look at the connections between your experience and others' experience and see what emerges from them. This objective position will give you a richer understanding of the situation. As your understanding grows, so the system is changed because your understanding is part of that system. So we have another interesting recursive loop.

Metaphors of Perspective

We naturally take perspectives when we want to gain a bet-ter understanding and it shows in our language:

'I can't see the wood for the trees.'
'I need to stand back and get the whole picture.'
'I'm too involved in this to know what to do.'
'I have to step back from this.'
'He is too caught up in his own agenda to know what to do.'
'I want to look at this close up.'
'If you were in his shoes, you would see it the same way.'
'Take a different angle on this.'

It is hard to change a system from an inside, subjective point of view only. You need to see the whole to judge whether your actions are having the desired effect. The outside view alone is also insufficient because it does not take into account the individual subjective meaning and importance of the issues to the people involved, This is why political actions, often with the best intentions, that are designed to get an overall result, often flounder because of local opposition.

Flat Earth Thinking or Global Thinking

Is the Earth flat? Obviously it is, just look beneath your feet. And yet, if the pictures from space are to be believed, it is round – and international travel confirms this every day. We know (or at least believe) the Earth is round, but for practical everyday purposes, we behave as if it is flat. Too often we actually become 'flat Earth thinkers', simplifying too much when we need to see the fuller picture.

A straight line is actually a partial arc – one part of a circle. It only looks flat because of our limited view. This brings us back to *punctuation* – how we make sense of these circles and sequences of events; indeed, whether we see beyond the lines at all to how they connect back to form circles. When you find yourself going round and round in circles in a pattern of miscommunication and blame it seems as though a straight line is taking you back to where you started. It is only when you can get an outside view of the system that you can see the circle and how to get out of it.

Punctuation is how we make sense of sequences.

Punctuation changes meaning in language and in experience.

Here's a great example of how punctuation makes a big difference:

Dear John,

I want a man who knows what love is all about. You are generous, kind, thoughtful. People who are not like you admit to being useless and inferior. You have ruined me for other men. I yearn for you. I have no feelings whatsoever when we're apart. I can be forever happy – will you let me be yours?

Gloria

Dear John

I want a man who knows what love is. All about you are generous, kind, thoughtful people who are not like you. Admit to being useless and inferior. You have ruined me. For other men I yearn. For you I have no feelings whatsoever. When we're apart I can be forever happy – will you let me be?

Yours, Gloria

Here is an example of how different punctuation changes experience. George and Jenny have been married for 10 years and have settled into a pattern that neither of them enjoys. Whenever they need to decide something important, they quarrel. Jenny says that George is too overbearing: 'He says what he thinks we should do and doesn't seem to pay any attention to what I think. And when I suggest some other possibilities he goes huffy and defensive. I wish he would be more open to what I have to say.'

Jenny reacts to George's pattern. Sometimes she even finds herself arguing the opposite point of view when she does not really agree with it, just to be different.

George has a different story. He says, 'Whenever we have a decision to make, it's always me who has to say what I think first. Jenny doesn't seem to know what she wants. But when I do give my point of view, she attacks it, I defend it and we both end up arguing. I wish she wouldn't attack my ideas.'

George reacts to Jenny's pattern despite himself.

In practice, if it seems as though you are continually forced to respond to someone else in a particular way and neither of you is deriving any benefit from the situation, look for the reinforcing feedback loop; in other words, look at how your actions are influencing the other person to respond in the way that you are reacting to. Is your reaction their trigger?

When you are inside an argument like this, it can go round and round for a long time (and for this couple, it did). From outside, it's a loop: George responding to Jenny responding to George. However, punctuate it differently. Jenny sees George as starting the rally (by putting forward his view regardless) and George sees Jenny as the instigator (by attacking his ideas). Starting anywhere, it is a reinforcing feedback loop. There is a further diabolical twist that keeps it in place – both expect the other to argue in a particular way, so both adopt their own way as an antidote. However, from the outside, it is not the antidote at all, but the malady. And the situation is undiscussible, which keeps the loop even more firmly in place. This like a game that has dreadful rules, but you have to keep playing because there are no rules about how or when the rules can be changed.

From the outside, both George and Jenny share the same mental model, that is, they both think they are responding to the other and it's the other who starts the ball rolling. So if only the other person would change then it would all be OK. Both have half the picture, but a half-truth can be as misleading as a lie.

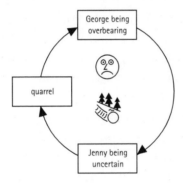

Punctuation in a domestic quarrel

The leverage point in this sort of quarrel is to step outside the loop and see the structure of the situation. So we ask the basic question: *What stops the situation changing?*

First, to keep the loop intact, both parties have to play. If one were to act differently, it would break the circle. Both George and Jenny are reacting to the other, so if one were to change, the other would have to as well. To make the change, one of them has to go outside the loop and question what is happening. Then they can shift the discussion to a different level. For example, Jenny could say, 'It seems to me that whenever we have a decision to make, we always end up arguing. What can we do that would help us to stop this?'

This has to be done carefully. If done during the course of an argument, George may simply put it in the same frame as the rest of the row. He could respond, 'There you go again, leaving it up to me...'

Taking a time out is essential. Often parties in these loops do try to step outside them, but all their outside observations are taken by the other party as part of the same loop. This is why an outside mediator is so useful, being by definition outside the loop to begin with.

Once you are outside the system, you have a chance to change it. What is the purpose of the conversation? From George's point of view it is to agree a decision. The same for Jenny. However, neither goal takes the *system* into account – their relationship. So both have to keep an extra goal in mind: to preserve or enhance their relationship.

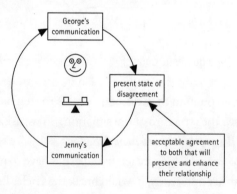

Balanced punctuation

These sorts of misunderstandings and quarrels can lead to very strong feelings that make them even harder to resolve. Here is another paradox – because it is unpleasant, both sides try to resolve the situation, but they try to do so by doing more of the very thing that is making the situation so unpleasant. The feelings are caused by the structure of the system. Neither person is to blame.

A Thought Experiment

You may be part of one of these unsatisfying loops where you and another person just seem to be reacting to what the other says or does, the situation never seems to resolve itself and both of you are dissatisfied. Try this experiment:

_____

Think of the situation.

From your point of view, label the other person's attitude and actions.

Now, make a leap of the imagination, and from the other person's point of view, label how you must appear to them, your attitude and actions as they appear to the other side. This may not be very flattering. It doesn't matter, it is one point of view and no more true of the total situation than yours.

Now take a mental step outside and imagine the two of you engaged in the situation, argument or conversation. Ask yourself some questions:

■ *What is the relationship between these two people during the argument?*

■ *What is that you, there, are doing that could be trig-
   gering the other person's response?*
■ *What are they doing that is triggering your response?*
■ *How does your response trigger their response?*
■ *What relationship do you want with the other person?*
■ *What response do you really want from them?*
■ *What could you do that would get that response?*
■ *If what you are doing at the moment is not working, what,
   if anything, stops you from doing something different?*

In the example, George and Jenny are responding, each in their
own way. Each evokes the behaviour of the other and complements
it. This is called a *complementary* relationship. A *symmetrical* relationship is when both parties evoke the same behaviour from the other.
For example, the angrier one person becomes, the angrier their
opponent becomes. These types of relationships can lead to escalating violence. The arms race between the Soviet Union and America
during the Cold War was an international example of a symmetrical
relationship: whenever America increased their spending on arms,
the Soviet Union felt threatened and did the same. And whenever
the Soviets increased their spending, America felt threatened and
responded in kind. From the Soviets' point of view, they were simply responding to provocation by America. From America's point
of view, the Soviet Union was continually increasing the level and
destructive power of their arms, so in self-defence, they had to as
well. Both countries considered they were acting in self-defence
and both considered the other the 'cause' of the trouble.

   A symmetrical relationship may escalate all the way to
violence, unless one party steps back from the brink or another
balancing loop comes into play (like fear!)

In a complementary relationship, the two parties are not in competition and they may not escalate the conflict, but just get stuck in a rut where neither is happy.

Both types of relationship, symmetrical and complementary, can be constructive or destructive, it depends on how the parties are relating, on exactly what behaviour they are evoking from the other. In practice, neither type of relationship is good if taken too far, as they fix roles too rigidly.

The Road to Hell

The limiting loops like the one between George and Jenny only run because each person has trapped themselves inside the system and only sees it from their own viewpoint. According to our own viewpoint, of course, what we do makes perfect sense. From another's point of view, it may look completely weird.

Simply taking the other person's view does not get you out of the loop because the other person's view is also within the system. As long as you are within the system and do not know it, there seems to be only two choices – to carry on as you are, or admit you are wrong and the other person is right.

In this system, neither person intends to quarrel, but the result is still an argument. Good intentions are not enough. As the saying goes, 'The road to hell is paved with good intentions.'

A further problem is that we tend to judge our own actions by our intentions. From our point of view, we do what is reasonable in the circumstances and if it goes wrong or hurts someone else, we excuse ourselves by saying we did not mean that to happen. We are innocent, unlucky or at worst thoughtless.

We judge others differently. Not seeing the world from their point of view, we do not judge them by their intentions but by their *results*, and we do not see the constraints they are under. If they hurt us, we assume they intended to, or at the very least were stupid and incompetent. Quite a contrast to the way we judge ourselves! We are mostly unaware that we are reacting to behaviour and not intentions. We think the meaning of our communication is what we intend, but take the meaning of the other person's communication as its effect on us. This is the road to the hell of misunderstanding and blame ... paved with good intentions.

What keeps this situation going? Mostly because it is all done silently within our own world. We rarely communicate what we feel. We imagine that if we told others of our judgements to their face, it would probably hurt them and make them defensive, and in turn we believe we would feel hurt and defensive were someone to do the same to us. So we keep quiet and this keeps the whole process hidden. In the absence of honest feedback, everyone continues down the same road.

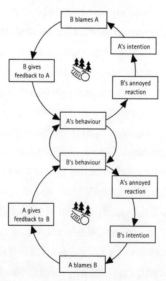

The road to hell – intention and blame

Take a look at the diagram. You are A and your loop is at the bottom. The more B engages in their obnoxious behaviour, the more you become annoyed and the less you credit their intentions as they see them. The less you understand their intentions, the more you blame them, and the more you blame them, the less likely you are to be honest with them, and so the more they are likely to continue doing whatever they are doing. The same process applies to B in response to your actions in the upper loop. The net result is the reinforcing loop in the middle – the more you make your response, the more they make theirs, and the more they make theirs, the more you respond with yours.

There are two leverage points. The first is in the bottom loop – break the link between your annoyed reaction and discounting the other person's intention. Act as if the other person's action makes perfect sense to them and is trying to get something of value for them in their world. You can then start to explore exactly what they want and find out if there are other ways they can get it without annoying you. The second is in the top loop, where you can sever the link between your behaviour and their interpretation.

Focus on what you want to achieve. Act as if the meaning of your behaviour is what the other person makes of it, use their feedback and be prepared to change what you do as necessary until you achieve the reaction you want. No one is going to understand you as well as you understand yourself.

SUMMARY: PART THREE

Learning

■ Learning is changing ourselves using the feedback from our
actions.
■ We learn from everything we do.
■ Learning is a balancing feedback loop. You take action, you
experience the results of those actions and you take decisions
based on those results, which lead to more actions. You
always have some purpose in mind.

SIMPLE LEARNING

■ Simple learning, or first order learning or adaptive learning, is
changing your response based on the feedback you get to
move you closer to your goal. There are two sorts of single
loop learning:
In time uses feedback in the moment.
Through time uses feedback to do better next time. There are
feedback loops not only within an action, but also in a series
of actions over time.

GENERATIVE LEARNING

■ Generative learning, or double loop learning, brings our mental models into the feedback loop.
■ It may either reinforce them or make us question them.

WHAT PREVENTS US LEARNING?

- deleting part of the feedback
- **dynamic complexity**
- limiting mental models
- difficulties in measuring feedback
- confusion between precision and accuracy
- setting thresholds for feedback that are either too high or too low
- not paying attention to the feedback from our senses
- not asking good questions

Perspectives

A perspective is a point of view.

Systems thinking looks at how experiences relate, how they go together to form greater wholes.

It is important to have many different perspectives to get as full a picture as possible and to widen our mental models.

The world is always richer than any representation we have of it.

There are two fundamental perspectives:

An objective view is looking at a system from outside it.

A subjective view is looking at a system from inside it.

Systems thinking uses both views.

Which view you adopt depends on how you define the boundary of the system you are considering.

There can never be final objectivity, because you can never stand completely outside the system of which you are a part.

■ The subjective perspective divides into:
your own perspective from the inside out
someone else's perspective

■ Your mental models, and those of others, are also part of the system.

PUNCTUATION

■ Punctuation is how we make sense of feedback loops and sequences of events.
■ Different punctuation starts from different places in the circle.
■ In a complementary relationship each person behaves differently and what they do fits together, each evoking the other's reaction.
■ In a symmetrical relationship both parties evoke the same behaviour from the other.

drawing conclusions

You can use systems thinking to literally draw your own conclusions. You can draw connections and feedback loops, and the system will take shape before your eyes. Then you can play with it, brainstorm connections, use it to think up, down and laterally. This is an intuitive way of working, because it is visual. Also, you are not only mapping the system 'out there', but your own understanding at the same time; you are drawing your own thought processes and will see your own mental models in your system diagram. That drawing will show your situation, how it was built and your assumptions about it.

When you draw a system, you will be drawing feedback loops to trace and understand how one component influences the others. You will build a number of closed, interacting feedback loops that encapsulate the most important influences.

How can you use a systems diagram to see the leverage points for changes and possible solutions? Just a few simple principles are needed and absolutely no mathematics are involved. Once you know how, you can use your diagram to identify leverage points, suggest changes and see immediately what effect they have. These changes may be external, 'out there' in the world, or they may be internal, in the way you are thinking.

Drawing a system is like telling a story in pictures. The story can be a romance, a historical novel, a thriller, a detective story or whatever you want. It may be mundane, exciting, tragic or comic. Some stories are perennial favourites, the plots cropping up in many different guises. If you have ever said to yourself, 'Why does this keep happening to me?' you will know the feeling. Some plots are complex, others are simple. None have guaranteed happy endings – you supply the ending. All of them take into account the two basic building blocks of systems – feedback loops and the relationships between different elements. We will use examples from health, business, finances and relationships, because all these aspects of your life have a story to tell.

Mapping your Intuitions

You are the hero, the protagonist of the story. It is *your* story, seen from *your* point of view. You are a part of it. What is your story about? What do you want? You need a clear goal in order to set the boundaries of the system, so first decide what it is. You may want to solve a business problem or to explore a health issue. You may want to understand a relationship better or explore how to expand your business.

Once you have chosen your theme, the next question is, what will be in your story? Every story has a start and a finish, and of all the details an author could put in, they write only what is needed. In your story, you decide the details, depending on what you believe is important. For example, suppose you are the manager of a high street store and you want to take a systems view of your business. You would start by listing those elements you see as the most important: location, staff, window display, local competition, stock, size of premises, prices, service, parking, store layout. This is a neutral list; how you use it and elaborate it depends on what you want to understand. You may want to attract more customers, find out why the customer base is declining or manage stock more efficiently. You define the situation or problem and what you believe is important determines the system boundary. Stay focused on the issue or you risk your story turning into a version of *War and Peace*. It is possible to set the boundary too wide in two ways:

■ By including unnecessary elements of a larger system. For example, including economic and political factors that influence the import of food when looking for a plan to lose weight.

■ By including elements from smaller subsystems. This would be like researching the neurotransmitters involved in the sensation of hunger when planning your diet.

Be sure you have enough of the right sort of pieces to make a coherent story.

Time is another sort of boundary. Take too short a time span and you risk missing important elements. When in doubt, err on the side of a longer time span so you can take into account possible time delays. Take a time span that is at least as long as the time taken for the issue to build up. It depends on what you want to understand. For example, changing business culture may take years. On the other hand, if you are looking at reorganizing a business department you need to consider how long it will take for actions in that department to radiate out into the whole business. Planning a sales campaign needs a time span of a few weeks. Changing your eating habits will need several months. Time is the dimension in which the elements of the system influence each other. The people involved are also important. Who will you include inside the boundary?

A system is a process. When you are dealing with systems, it does not matter where you start. All the pieces are connected, so wherever you start will give you the feedback loops. You do not need to worry that you have started in the 'wrong' place.

So, once you know why you are looking at your system, begin with the events you experience and believe are important. These events will form a pattern, they have a meaning. Look out for repeated events of the same type. This is a strong clue that there is a system structure operating that keeps running in the same way. As already mentioned, an isolated experience is just that – and can mean whatever we want it to mean – and the same experience twice *may* be a coincidence, but three times is a pattern. One quarrel is an event. Repeated quarrels are a pattern. Missing a deadline once is bad luck. Repeatedly missing them is a pattern. Be suspicious of runs of misfortune, or a row of coincidences, or continually finding yourself with the same problem, even if each time there is a different, plausible explanation.

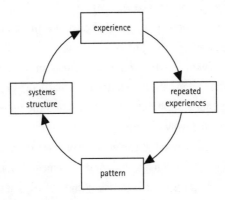

Experience and pattern

At the event level, you may have little influence. But once you perceive the pattern, you can draw a system structure and from this you can look for the leverage points that will change the structure and therefore change your experience.

The next principle is to use elements that increase or decrease in your system diagram. If an element cannot change, then by definition, it cannot be influenced. If you find an element in your system drawing that does not change, think about what it represents or what it gets for you. For example, if an object like your house comes into the picture, it might

drawing conclusions

represent comfort, safety, a financial asset or a way of raising money. Exactly what it represents will depend on what you are exploring with your drawing.

Guidelines for Drawing Systems

1. You are the central character in the situation. Draw from your experience and your viewpoint.
2. Draw with a goal in mind. What do you want to understand?
3. Start wherever you want.
4. Include events – what you observe, hear and feel. Those that repeat or seem to form a pattern are particularly significant.
5. Define your system boundaries, including the time span and the people involved, depending on your goal.
6. Only use elements that can increase or decrease, so can change when they are influenced by another element. If you want to use something that is fixed, ask, 'What does this get for me?'

Storytime

The first basic plot is the reinforcing loop. This is like a snow-ball rolling down the hill, the bigger it gets – the bigger it gets. Below is a simple example of a reinforcing loop: the larger the sales force (up to a point), the more sales made. The more sales, the more the company grows and the larger the sales force becomes.

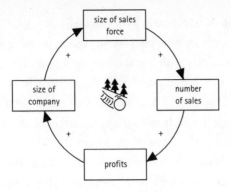

Now we will look more closely at the links between the elements. Notice the first link. The larger the sales force, the more sales are made. The smaller the sales force, the fewer sales are made. Both elements change in the same direction. An increase in one leads to an increase in the other. A decrease in one leads to a decrease in the other. This is a reinforcing link. All the links in this example are this type of reinforcing link. It is known as a *proportional* link – the two elements move in proportion to each other.

There is a second type of reinforcing link. This is when a change in one element simply adds to the next element. Take a look at the diagram.

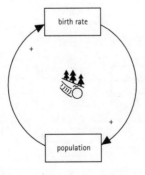

Population loop

drawing conclusions

This is another reinforcing loop – overall it grows, everything else being equal (as time goes on, of course, limiting factors will come into play with any reinforcing loop). Notice the link between birth rate and population. An increase in birth rate adds to the population, but a decrease in birth rate does not subtract from the population. It still adds to it, but more slowly. In other words, unlike the last type of reinforcing link, the two elements do not always move in the same direction. When the birth rate increases, so does the population, but when the birth rate decreases, the population may still rise, but less than before. This is called an *additive reinforcing link*. An increase in one element adds to the other regardless. All reinforcing links, both additive and proportional, are shown with a positive sign. This does not mean they are good; the sign simply stands for a reinforcing link.

Now look at the following diagram. This is an example of a reinforcing loop for a tennis player.

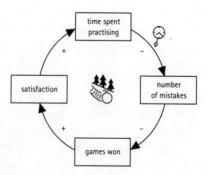

Reinforcing loop

Overall the loop is reinforcing. Notice the links. The more time spent practising, the fewer mistakes, the less time spent practising, the more mistakes. So these two elements change in the opposite direction (an increase in one leads to a decrease in the other and vice versa). This is a proportional balancing link shown by the negative sign next to the arrow. The negative sign does not mean it is bad in any way. All balancing links are shown with negative signs. The next link is also a balancing link. The fewer mistakes, the more games won, the more mistakes, the fewer games won. The following two links are both reinforcing – the more games won, the more satisfaction, and the more satisfaction, the more motivation to practise. The whole sequence forms a reinforcing feedback loop, even though it has balancing links within it. When you imagine travelling round the loop, taking a skill you have learnt, your experience will confirm it is reinforcing.

There is a simple rule that will let you know whether the complete loop is reinforcing or balancing, regardless of the number or the type of links. If the whole sequence has an even number of negative (balancing) links, then it will be a reinforcing loop (and that includes those loops where there are no balancing links, because zero is an even number). If it has an odd number of negative (balancing) links, it will be a balancing loop. The reason is that two negative links will cancel out and form the equivalent of a reinforcing link (for example in the diagram, more practice leads to more games being won).

It is also possible to have another sort of balancing link – where one element subtracts from the other. Fishing is an example.

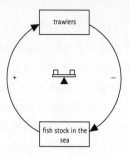

Fishing

The more trawlers, the fewer fish in the sea. However, fewer trawlers do not mean more fish stocks. Any number of trawlers simply subtracts from the number of fish in the sea, so it always makes it less. It is a balancing link.

The second basic plot is the balancing loop. All balancing loops have goals. What drives a balancing loop is the attempt to close the gap between actual performance or experience and the target or goal. This leads to action, perhaps successful, perhaps not.

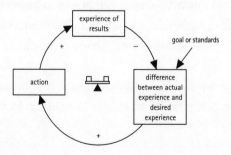

Balancing loop

When we eliminate the difference, there is no more action and no more loop. In practice, we may not close the gap completely because of limits imposed by other factors. The standards we have and the goals we set determine the degree of difference between what we want and what we are getting and therefore the amount of effort we put into closing the gap. The higher the standard, the bigger the gap and the greater the effort needed to close it.

We have resisted the temptation to simplify this section, because we think it would be misleading. It would soon become obvious to you that there are two kinds of balancing links and two kinds of reinforcing links because some links do not run backwards. The reason is this. There can be two kinds of elements in these systems drawings (causal loop diagrams) – a level and a flow.

A level is a quantity that accumulates over time, for example, population, number of people in a family, fish in the sea, money in a bank account. These are all levels.

A flow is a measurement of change over time. So birth rate, expenditure, usage of natural resources are all flows. A flow is always a movement. Anything that represents a 'rate' is a flow. So the amount of money in a bank account is a level and expenditure is a flow. The amount of beer in a glass is a level and the rate of beer pouring in from the tap is a flow. Flows lead to a change in a level. Both levels and flows can rise or fall. (For example, the population of a country can rise or fall and so can the birth rate.)

When you link a level to a level, then both are likely to change proportionately to each other in both directions.

drawing conclusions

However, linking a rate to a level will not change proportionately because even if a rate decreases, it will still be adding to the level, which will then rise.

For example, the link between birth rate (flow) and population (level) is a reinforcing one. When birth rate increases, so does population. However, when birth rate stays the same, the population still increases. Also, when birth rate declines, the population may still increase (if the death rate is low), because a falling birth rate still adds people to the level of the population. Or think of filling a glass with water – the greater the flow of water into the glass, the higher the water level. But if the rate of flow goes down, the amount in the glass does not go down, it continues to rise, but not as fast. So this gives us a second kind of reinforcing link where one element (flow) *adds* to the other (level). And the other kind of balancing link where one element (flow) *subtracts* from the other (level).

When there is no rate to level link, then the loops may be vicious or virtuous because both variables will move up or down together (for example, team morale and success), giving proportional links. When there are rate to level links, then the links will be additive (reinforcing) or subtractive (balancing).

This means we have to define our types of feedback links quite carefully to be completely accurate:

■ The first element has a reinforcing influence on the second when an increase (decrease) in the first results in the second becoming larger (smaller) than it would have been if the first had not changed.

■ The first element has an opposing or balancing influence on the second when an increase (decrease) in the first results in the second becoming smaller (larger) than it would have been if the first had not changed.

In practice this means you have to trace the elements carefully and use your knowledge and intuition. Causal loop diagrams do not differentiate between levels and flows. They do not need to. Follow the influence of one element on another by talking it through:

- If I increase X, what happens to Y?
- If Y also increases, it is a reinforcing link.
- If Y decreases, it is a balancing link.

This gives you the *structure* of the system. When you are actually looking at the *behaviour* of the system, you will need to look at exactly what sort of reinforcing and balancing links they are.

Systems drawings are one way to bring out the structure of a system. They will clarify many situations. However, it is not always easy to see how the system will *behave*. So the same behaviour can be produced by different structures and one structure can give rise to different forms of behaviour. Do not assume that the same structure always produces the same behaviour. The drawings are simplified models, they do not give cut and dried answers. It would be extraordinary if they did. They are not like mathematical formulae that always give the 'right' answer – there are no 'right' answers, only a series of possible answers that you can explore. (For a good discussion of this topic *see* 'Problems with causal loop diagrams' by George Richardson and Colleen Lannon in *The Systems Thinker* 7, 10, December 1996; available from Pegasus Communications, *see* Resources for address.)

Finally, put in the time delays that are significant, relative to the time scale of the rest of the diagram. We have used a small clock icon to do this. Time delays are nearly always important in understanding how the system will behave. In the tennis diagram, it takes time for practice to improve your game so you make fewer mistakes. Time delays mean that results come through slowly in comparison with the next link, like a factory production line where one piece of machinery is significantly slower than the rest. The slowest point will determine the overall speed and it is useless working faster with the other machines to try to overcome the bottleneck. In our practice example, we may work hard and experience no improvement at all. We might get disheartened, but if we persevere, what often happens is a sudden leap, as if all the work has reached a critical threshold, and we seem to become significantly better almost overnight. Time delays also ensure that the effects of what you do will continue for some time after you have stopped doing it.

Time delays can lead to a build up of pressure, just like a faulty valve in the system pipeline. When you think nothing is happening, you may crank up the pressure and this can lead to burnout. If the time delay is a long one relative to the rest of the system and the pressure keeps piling on, it will reach a threshold and the link will suddenly collapse. For example, junior doctors may be able to work two or three 80-hour weeks, but eventually the pressure is liable to be too much. They cannot continue such a schedule indefinitely.

Labelling your Systems Drawings

1 If a change in one element leads to a change in the next in the same direction (increase one and the other increases, decrease one and the other decreases), indicate this with a positive sign (+). This is a proportional reinforcing link. Also if one element simply adds to the other regardless, then this is also a reinforcing link, to be indicated by a positive sign.

2 If a change in one element leads to a change in the other in the opposite direction (increase one and the other decreases, or decrease one and the other increases), indicate this with a negative sign (–). This is a proportional balancing link. Also if one element simply subtracts from the other, then this is also a balancing link, to be indicated by a negative sign.

3 Show the character of the total feedback loop. In this book, a snowball indicates a reinforcing loop, a pair of scales shows a balancing loop.

4 A sequence with an even number of balancing links will give a reinforcing feedback loop (and zero is an even number). A sequence with an odd number of balancing links will be a balancing feedback loop.

5 Indicate any time delays that are significant relative to the rest of the diagram. In this book we will use a clock icon.

6 We have added some happy and sad faces. These are just our reaction to what is happening in the system, not part of the structure. We like them.

Now you know the basics of systems drawings. These drawings are called *causal loop diagrams*, or CLDs. They help you understand the structure of the system. Follow them round to see how the structure will behave and how the story will unfold. Time delays and different sorts of loops can connect in many different ways, so your creativity and artistry are still needed to make sense of the story and bring it to a satisfactory end.

Here are some examples to experiment with. Draw a loop and trace the influences round the loop. (NB. There are no right or wrong answers.)

■ Criticism makes me...
■ Stress makes me...
■ A sense of well-being makes me...
■ Time pressure makes me...
■ High petrol prices cause...
■ Earning more money means I...
■ Better customer service means...
■ Exercising makes me...

Running on the Spot

It has been said that all stories revolve around half a dozen basic themes. System stories, however complicated they seem, are all made from two links: balancing and reinforcing. These are combined to make more complex stories and after a while you will notice common themes in these stories. These themes are often called *archetypes* in systems literature. Archetype comes from the Greek and means an original model. Systems archetypes are basic patterns of events. Once you see the pattern, you will find them everywhere.

For example, have you ever been in a situation where you start getting good results but after a while they tail off? You keep pushing but you seem to be getting less and less result for more and more effort. This can be very frustrating. In the end you may be running on the spot simply to stay where you are. Your performance declines while your efforts go up.

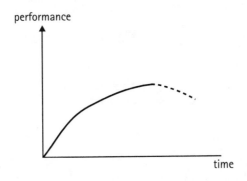

This story happens all the time. When we learn a skill for the first time we usually make rapid progress, but after a while it becomes much harder to maintain the same rate of improvement. This is why it is so hard to reach the very top of a profession – the last few steps are the hardest. Another example, this time from the medical field: initially a drug may be very successful in treating an illness, but after a while, resistant strains of bacteria emerge, the drug is less successful and new drugs are developed. In a business, a marketing campaign may initially gain many customers, but subsequent campaigns may meet with less and less success as the market becomes saturated. And your bank manager is likely to become less and less forthcoming the more often you go to ask for a loan.

drawing conclusions

What is happening? In systems terms, the same basic structure is responsible for stopping an epidemic and putting a ceiling on achievement – a reinforcing loop has met a balancing
loop. We welcome this decline when the reinforcing loop is taking us in a vicious, downwards spiral, but wish it away when it
limits the results we are working for.

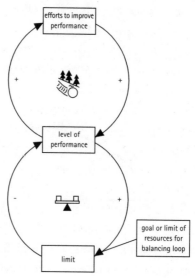

Limits to success pattern

This structure is known as the 'limits to success' pattern. Initially,
the greater the effort, the better the performance. And the better
the performance, the more we are encouraged to keep up the
effort. Then success meets some limit. The greater the success
the more the limit operates, and the more the limit operates, the
more performance declines. It is as if when you put your foot on
the accelerator, the brake comes on too. More of the same effort
will not solve the problem. For example, we have both been

guilty as trainers of carrying on a training session too long. Encouraged by how much the participants were learning and enjoying the training, we kept adding to the material. After a while, the participants tired and their attention wandered, and it was tempting to carry on and try to help them recapture that first enthusiasm. Wrong. They needed a break.

You may have been on the receiving end of something like that. Joseph recently spent a day as a trainee that lasted from eight o'clock in the morning to eight o'clock in the evening with half an hour official break for lunch. By mid-afternoon, many of the participants were taking extended 'unofficial' breaks and grumbling about the training. The limit to learning was the attention and the energy of the participants.

There are many business examples of this principle. A very successful business can create a situation where they are taking so many orders that delivery times lengthen and quality declines. Customers become dissatisfied and then orders decrease. Another example is the computer hardware industry. Processor speeds double roughly every two years according to Moore's Law. But computer hardware on its own is useless. It needs software. So one of the limits on hardware design and computer operating systems is the software available and how easily it will run. Good hardware on its own is not enough. And in the last analysis, the consumer decides how well software runs.

Sometimes the limit is simple: it is impossible to grow any more. There is a limit to how tall trees can grow before they topple over. There are limits to how big a company can grow, given its level of turnover. There are always thresholds. An amusing instance of this happened a few years ago when a large hangar was built at Cape Kennedy to protect the space shuttle from the Florida thunderstorms. The hangar was huge. So huge, in fact, that it generated its own weather system from the currents of warm and cold air that circulated within it. It was generating more of the very problem it was built to solve.

When you hear these sorts of phrases, you can be confident that this limiting structure is operating:

■ 'It used to be so easy...'
■ 'It's not the same any more.'
■ 'Why can't it be as easy as it was?'
■ 'It's harder and harder to get the same result these days.'
■ 'I just seem to spending all my energy running on the spot.'
■ 'However hard I work, I never seem to be getting anywhere.'
■ 'The glory days are over...'
■ 'Why aren't we doing as well as we used to?'
■ 'There seems to be a glass ceiling on this.'
■ 'Let's fight our way out of trouble.'

Limits to Natural Resources

This pattern of a growing loop meeting a limit in a balancing loop happens on both a large and a small scale. Standards of living steadily rise and then slow down. There are limited natural resources to fuel economic growth.

The clearest examples of this pattern come from the limits to growth that are imposed by natural resources. For example, population growth and manufacturing capability depend on adequate supplies of water. There is a world-wide exponential demand for water and it is growing faster than the available supply. Water supplies can be increased by building dams to trap rivers and floodwater, and by building desalination plants. The water can be widely distributed through long-distance pipelines. However, there are limits.

Pollution is one. In a year it renders almost as much water unusable as is utilized by the whole world economy. Another limit comes from local political opposition to the building of dams and desalination plants. Even if it were possible to trap all rainfall for human use and stop all water pollution, we would reach the limit on available water given our present exponentially growing rate of use in about 100 years, so in reality we will meet it very much sooner. No present technology can put off this fateful day. The shortages will not be distributed equally – some countries will be very short of water, others may have enough for their needs. Water could be the oil of the next century.

The limits of natural resources suggest three simple rules for sustainable rates of use:[1]

- ■ *A renewable resource* (for example animals, fish, soil, water, forests) should not be used at a greater rate than the rate at which it can regenerate itself.
- ■ *A non-renewable resource* (for example mineral ore, fossil fuels) should not be used more quickly than a renewable resource used in a sustainable way can be substituted for it.
- ■ *A pollutant* (a toxic, non-usable by-product, for example nuclear waste, sewage) should not be produced faster than it can be recycled, neutralized or absorbed by the environment.

We are not using resources at the moment at sustainable rates. Therefore we will meet limits. The only question is when.

Examples of the limits to success pattern:

drawing conclusions

- the human ageing process
- economic growth followed by decline
- infectious disease epidemics petering out
- the slowing of the growth of a new business
- losing weight rapidly at the start of a diet, then more slowly
- learning a skill quickly at the beginning, then less easily
- the initial excitement of courting a new sexual partner
  gradually fading

Inner and Outer Limits

Where are the leverage points in this story of limits to success? There are three.

The first is to look for limits early. Nothing can grow forever, so you can prepare for the limits while still improving rapidly. In a business, a relationship, a new skill, a network of friends or your career, plan ahead for the possible limits. The limits may be material resources, people, money, beliefs, standards, energy or traditions. Prepare at the start by asking two questions:

- 'What limits am I likely to encounter?'
- 'What can I do as I grow to simultaneously increase my ability to handle these limits when they arrive?'

The time when you are growing and improving is precisely the time to prepare for problems. When improvement slows, do not keep doing the same thing, for the slowing down is a signal to change to a different strategy. Best of all, start to use the different strategy *before* you need to. If you wait until you need to, it may be too late.

When there is a delay in the system, you will keep growing for a time, even when you switch resources into another strategy. So open a new business market while the old one is still booming. The Virgin group is an example of a company that did well in its original niche, in its case music, but has expanded into many new fields – publishing, travel and financial services – without waiting for peak performance in any one field. Poor performance with the new market should be at least as good as excellent performance in the old system. The areas of your greatest success will be the very areas where you will have to rethink your strategy.

The second leverage point comes from asking the basic systems question *'What is limiting me?'* The answer is the balancing loop. So one answer is to remove or weaken this constraint, not push harder on the reinforcing loop.

It is very tempting to push harder with the old strategy. But beware of doing more of what worked in the past, or doing it harder. When you look at the system you will see that the balancing loop *uses your own energy* to resist you. It is using your own strength to trap you. It reminds us of those woven hollow tubes known as finger traps. You put your right index finger in one end and your left index finger in the other end. Then the harder you try to pull them apart, the more the material grips them tight. The only way to get out is to do the opposite of common sense – relax and push your finger in further. This loosens the hold and allows you to gently extract your fingers.

There is another trap too. When business performance deteriorates, it is tempting to hold back investment in those areas.

However, it may be that investment in new training, equipment or production capacity is what is needed to get past the restraint. Without new investment, performance may decline further and this decline be used to justify the decision not to invest – an interesting example of an undesired effect being used to justify its cause!

The third leverage point is in the mental models behind your actions. The idea of headlong expansion may lead to unsustainable growth. Consider these questions:

■ Is growth always a good thing?
■ What will this increased growth or experience get for you?
■ Is there another way to get it?
■ Is bigger necessarily better?
■ Do you want sustainable growth?
■ How far ahead are you looking for the effects?

All systems, particularly living systems, have an optimum point where they work best. Pushing for growth may lead to collapse by putting too much pressure on other parts of the system.

Weight Control

Dieting and weight control show the limits to success story in full flight. Here, success is losing weight. How does a diet work from a systems point of view? Weight is an emergent property –

it is not just inert stuff, but a tangible, visible sign of your body's metabolism. Western culture has elevated body weight into something more – an icon by which to judge health, beauty and self-esteem. The whole area is fraught with uncertainty, and the importance of weight to health is obscured by all kinds of cosmetic and emotional issues.

Obesity, for instance, is not the same as weight. Obesity is an accumulation of fat beyond what is considered normal for a person's age, sex and body type. This is a cultural mental model. Normal fat levels are presently defined as 20 per cent for men and 30 per cent for women. So obesity is nothing to do with how much you weigh, it is about how much of your weight is fat. It is possible, though not common, to be underweight and still obese. Muscle weighs more than fat, so fitness training may actually increase your weight, because it increases your muscle mass. The scales are not the best measurement of a healthy weight. What is needed is a method to measure the percentage of body fat.

When a person diets, they usually lose the first few pounds very easily. These will be mostly water and glycogen. Glycogen is a form of glucose stored in the muscles and the liver, and provides the most immediately available form of energy. Lack of glycogen can lead to low blood sugar, resulting in depression, tiredness and irritability. Here is the first hurdle for the dieter to overcome. After this initial weight loss, it becomes increasingly difficult. The balancing loop that limits the initial success arises from your body's metabolic rate – how fast you burn the calories you eat. When you eat less food, your body, intelligent system that it is, adjusts by lowering your metabolic rate after a time delay. The lower metabolic rate adjusts to the lower food intake and you stop losing weight. The prime leverage point is to increase your metabolic rate through exercise while reducing calorie intake.

Does this mean the more exercise you do, the faster your metabolic rate and the more efficiently you lose weight? No. There is a limit to the success of exercise (wouldn't you have guessed it?) Intense and prolonged exercise increases your appetite and so makes dieting more difficult. It also weakens your immune system, making you more prone to illness.

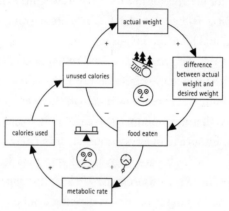

Dieting – limits to success

The desired weight is another leverage point. It is not government appointed, it varies dramatically from person to person. Your desired weight comes from your experience of your own health and well-being and it is a mental model. You can review it at any time. The lower the desired weight, the more pressure there is on the top reinforcing loop.

There are other possibilities too. The amount of food you eat depends on your appetite. The drug Silutramine has been undergoing intensive trials in Europe; it fools the brain into thinking the stomach is full, so you eat less, which helps the top reinforcing loop. However, it leaves the balancing loop untouched. There are also chemicals known as thermogenic agents that will increase the metabolic rate and so weaken the balancing loop. Caffeine is one and nicotine is another; both, of course, have side-effects. It might be better to be slightly overweight than become a coffee-addicted chain smoker. Other foods are being developed that satisfy the appetite without supplying many calories. Olestra is a fat substitute developed in America, but once again there are side-effects; in this case it can act as an unpredictable laxative. There are always side-effects, particularly in such an exquisitely complex system as the human body.

It is not surprising that in the long run, most dieters gain weight, for two reasons. First, the body has not been getting as much fat as it used to and becomes more efficient at storing fat. It stays efficient for some time after the diet ends.

Second, after losing glycogen and water, the body loses next what it needs least, and if you are not very active, that will be lean muscle tissue of the sort that normally burns unwanted calories. This loss slows the metabolic rate still further and strengthens the bottom balancing loop. Medical studies have shown that the body is still trying to return to its initial weight even after four years.[2]

These dynamics can lead to a cycle of dieting, losing weight quickly, then putting the weight back on. Weight fluctuates, dropping during the diet and climbing back and beyond when dieting stops. The limiting factor is the person's metabolic rate, which takes time to adjust to the new calorie intake.

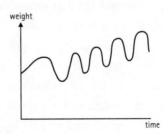

Weight-time oscillation

Moving the Goal Posts

A balancing loop is driven by the difference between where you are and where you want to be. The system works to decrease the difference by moving the present state towards the desired state, given that the desired state is fixed. However, there is another way to close the gap – lower the standards and bring the desired state closer.

This can be a useful move. For example, setting a body weight that is realistic and comfortable for the person you are. Some goals are totally unrealistic and benefit from a drastic overhaul. For example, an anorexic's ideal body image is not realistic and drives them to semi-starvation. Part of the treatment is to change that body ideal. We also know businessmen who are driven by unrealistic standards of perfection, not in body weight, but in business goals. A loop can become an endless, exhausting tread-mill if your best is never good enough, because an external or internal goal is not realistic. At other times, though, lowering goals may be used as an expedient way of excusing a disappoint-ing performance.

There are two ways that goals can drift downwards. First, goals may become set by current performance, rather than the current performance being set by goals, and this can lead to continuous stagnation rather than continuous improvement. A previously unacceptable level of performance may become the norm. Habituation is a sign of drifting goals if we now tolerate what was previously intolerable. It can happen on a national scale with levels of unemployment or inflation. It can happen in business – for example, a manufacturing company may pride itself on delivering its product within a week. Ten days is not acceptable. Gradually, this slips so that 10 days *is* an acceptable time, sometimes even two weeks. When delivery takes two weeks, customers complain vociferously, so a new goal is set for a 10-day delivery. This is the story of the British post office when they introduced first-class and second-class letter delivery. Previously, people expected their letters to arrive the next day. The newly introduced first-class delivery service promised what was previously taken as normal – next day delivery – but it cost slightly more. Gradually, the goal of next day delivery even for first-class post drifted. Now, guaranteed next day delivery is an extra service and it costs more again.

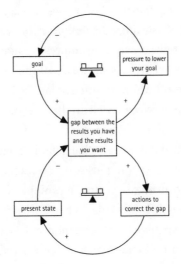

Drifting goals

Here is the drifting goals archetype. The bottom balancing loop describes the actions we take to reduce the gap between what we have and what we want. The downwards drift in the goals comes from the top balancing loop. The gap between what we want and what we have creates pressure to lower the goal instead of striving to achieve it. The greater the pressure, the more the goal is likely to be lowered.

drawing conclusions

Our personal goals may drift when we settle for a lower level of health and well-being than we want.

A slow downwards drift is not easy to see at the time, because we become used to the status quo. Businesses do not hear the alarm bells ring if their performance deteriorates over months rather than weeks. A small change may go unnoticed, but looking back, many small changes over time add up to one big change.

The second way goals can drift is more devious: the goal is creatively redefined. For example, when a high level of unemployment is causing political difficulties, an easy way to reduce unemployment is to change the definition of who counts as unemployed. A railway can show impressive figures for trains running on time, if a train is allowed a 10-minute period of grace before it is officially classified as late. Parts of the British National Health Service may claim that everyone is seen within 10 minutes, but this is cold comfort if 'being seen' means having your name taken and being given an appointment, then waiting three hours to see a doctor. This sort of reframing makes comparisons of performance over time meaningless.

Goals can also drift upwards. When a sales target is reached easily, it may be set higher the next month. Upwards drift can be dangerous, for example when a person's definition of 'social drinking' escalates to dozens of bottles of wine and spirits every week and their increasing tolerance of alcohol prevents them feeling the harm done to themselves and their family.

In systems terms, the greater the gap between actual and desired performance, the greater the temptation to lower, or creatively redefine, the goal. The more the goal is lowered, the more the gap between actual and desired state is reduced – 'no problem is too big to run away from'.

How can we prevent this? Goals drift when current standards are set by past performances rather than a vision of the future. A standard that is set *outside* the system is some protection against goals drifting upwards or downwards, for example, industry bench-marking for business or the advice of someone you trust for your personal goals.

Credit and Debt

Personal finances are often hard to control and our available cash flow sometimes seems to take on a will of its own. What system stories are at work?

Here's one possible story. A person finds they are short of money, so they rein in their spending. After a while they regain their financial balance and even have a little surplus. So they return to their previous spending and may perhaps splash out a little on something extra. A few months later they find themselves in debt again.

This common theme can turn into a horror story if the financial seesaw takes the person lower and lower every time, and it takes longer and longer to get back out of debt. The balance point of the seesaw can also slide downwards, so the high spot is merely less debt and not a credit balance. The story can take a further turn for the worse if the person starts to borrow on credit cards to meet the debt. This adds more debt still in the form of interest. There is a slippery slope that leads downwards into ever-increasing debt and possible bankruptcy.

If you have ever wondered why your finances do not stay completely stable, despite your best efforts, and what you can do the keep them more steady, then think of them as a system story.

Personal spending is a balancing loop driven by the gap between two forces. First, your desired standard of living –

the standard of material comfort and quality of life you expect. Second, your actual standard of living. The larger the gap between the two, the greater the temptation to spend in order to make up the gap. And there are limits – the funds available from your savings and income. The more we spend, the fewer available funds we have.

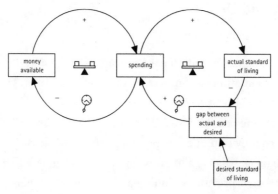

Personal finances

There are two balancing loops here, the first balancing spending and available money, the second trying to close the gap between what we have and what we want. The pressure is on the money available. When money available goes into the red, we cut spending. After a time delay, this feeds back to make more money available. The time delay means that we do not feel the effects of the cut in spending until later. Then all seems well again and the second balancing loop kicks in, putting pressure on money available. We feel the pinch from this next bout of spending after a delay and the cycle starts again. The art of managing personal finances is to balance these two loops. Often we forget the second loop (driven by the gap between what we have and what we want) and try to deal with the first loop (balancing money available against spending) in isolation.

There are two leverage points, one in each loop.

In the first loop, you can increase the money available. There are three ways to do this. First, by drawing on savings. The problem here is that if the second loop continues to operate as usual, the savings will be exhausted and you will go back to square one because the total system structure will not have changed. There are also side-effects. Reduced savings make you more vulnerable to emergencies and unplanned expenses. You no longer have a safety net. You may never want to have to use one, of course, but it does make you feel a lot better when it is there.

The second way to increase available money is to increase your real income by taking another or different job, getting promoted to a more highly paid post, or robbing banks. The first two can be good moves. The third has unpleasant legal consequences.

The third way to increase available funds is to use credit cards to borrow money. 'Buy today, pay tomorrow' is an attractive slogan, but what happens tomorrow? The more you borrow on credit cards, the more money you have available (today, anyway). The more money available, the more spending, and the more spending, the more you may have to borrow. This is an extra reinforcing loop above and beyond regular income. There is also a balancing loop. The more money borrowed, the greater the debt and the more the interest on the debt. The more the interest, the less money you have available. The extra interest is an extra burden that cannot be maintained in the long run if there are no extra resources in the system.

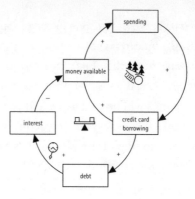

Credit card borrowing

Look at the credit card system diagram. On the surface, it looks as if we have simply added to our funds available by borrowing money and repaying it over time, but look deeper. This is only true if we repay the debt in full each month and incur no interest charges. The problem is the time delay between spending and the credit card bill. What can happen is that our attention is shifted from paying off the total debt to paying off the minimum monthly repayments. It seems as if we have more money to spend than we actually do, but credit cards do not increase the money you have available, although they are marketed as if they do. They let you spend *your* future money now and pay for the privilege. *You are borrowing from your future self* (who, if paying interest on the debt, has *less* money than you have now), but you pay interest to the credit card company. The debt in the present is caused by spending in the past. To borrow money in order to get out of debt is risky because interest payments increase the debt and this can set up a vicious reinforcing loop where borrowing to get out of debt increases the debt. Credit card interest grows exponentially. The larger the debt becomes, the quicker it grows. And we do not earn money exponentially!

The basic leverage point is in the balancing loop where spending is driven by the gap between the actual and desired standard of living. By reducing the desired standard of living we can drain the pressure from the system. So this is another example where letting a goal drift downwards can be a good move. We need to set up a balancing feedback loop in the first diagram between money available and desired standard of living. Also, your desired standard of living goal can be put into the future, it does not have to be experienced right now. A standard of living is not a fixed yardstick, but an ongoing experience of well-being by meeting your needs and the needs of those you care for.

It may be possible to get this feeling of well-being in other ways that do not involve spending more money. There are many pressures that lead us to expect standards of living will continue rising forever. But as systems thinkers we know this is impossible. There is also pressure to move our standards upwards because we soon get used to a set level of comfort and spending and start to set our sights higher. On a global level using scarce resources to fuel an ever-higher standard of living is the equivalent of running up a global credit card debt where we borrow from our children and leave them the debt *and* the interest payments.

In the long run, the only viable solutions are to increase your income (while attending to the systemic consequences in the rest of your life, i.e. how it affects your health and well-being and your valued leisure time) or to alter the mental model that creates the gap between actual and desired standard of living that drives the whole cycle.

Repairing the Damage, Again and Again...

Borrowing to get out of debt is an example of a very familiar story – when attempts to solve a problem only work temporarily and the problem returns just the same or worse the next time. Last winter, some friends of ours noticed mould was growing on a patch of kitchen wall near the floor. They wiped it off. It grew again. They wiped it off again. Still it returned. They increased the ventilation in the kitchen, thinking it was due to condensation on the cold wall, but this did not solve the problem either. Grumbling about mutant supermould, they wiped it off with fungicide. It grew back, but not so quickly. They decided desperate measures were called for and stripped the wallpaper off that wall, applied a coat of sealant paint directly onto the plaster and repapered. A few months later, the mould had appeared in a different place and the plaster had started to crumble. They replastered the faulty wall, but the wall stayed wet and the plaster continued to deteriorate. Eventually they called in a builder. The damp proof course had broken down and a new one had to be laid. The wall also had to be plastered again. Once done, the ground water did not rise up the wall and the new plaster stayed dry. In the end, the short-term fixes had not solved the problem but had made it worse, because the plaster was deteriorating the whole time.

Our decisions have both short and long-term consequences. In the short term we may solve the problem. In the long term we may be leaving it unchanged or even making it worse. The system will let you know, because if the problem persists, then the fundamental cause is still active. It is rather like having a fuse repeatedly blow in the main fuse box. A blown fuse is a warning, not just an annoyance. You can repair the fuse or trace the fault in the electrical circuit. The worst choice would be to put in a much higher rated fuse. Some years ago, a friend was looking at a flat where the previous tenant had put together a makeshift plug for his electric fire, bound it together with insulating tape and then replaced the fuse in the old-fashioned fuse box with a metal nail, presumably because the proper fuse kept on blowing. They were lucky to leave the flat alive. Unless you repair the system fault, the pressure will come through at the weakest point.

Here is a business example. The London office of an international advertising agency wanted to make the firm more competitive by cutting costs. They looked at their salary bill and saw they could make immediate substantial savings by making two senior copywriters redundant. This they did. These two men were very creative and were immediately taken on by a competitor. While the agency were successful in cutting costs, in the long run they became less competitive. Without two of their best writers their reputation fell. They lost work to their competitor. To make matters worse, losing the two best workers lowered morale in the whole firm. Soon the company was under pressure again and decided they had to make savings – by cutting salaries...

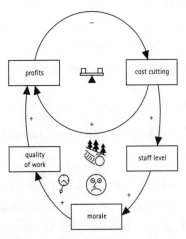

Short-term fix – long-term problem

In this story the balancing loop is trying to solve the problem, but unforeseen side-effects are creating a reinforcing loop which is either creating the very problem they are trying to solve or making it worse. This is known as the 'fixes that fail' archetype.

When you fix a problem but it keeps returning, you can be fairly confident that you are a victim of this system structure. It comes from focusing too much on the short term. Ask yourself, what are the unintended consequences of the fix that could be adding to the problem? A short-term fix is only useful as a stop gap until the fundamental cause can be tackled.

To escape from this story, two things are necessary. First, acknowledge that the short-term fix is not really working, and second, discover and tackle the underlying problem now.

Look for this story when you hear these sorts of phrases:

- ■ 'I thought I had dealt with this problem.'
- ■ 'This keeps turning up like a bad penny.'
- ■ 'This problem is getting to be a habit.'
- ■ 'Why won't this problem go away?'
- ■ 'Not this again!'
- ■ 'Can't you fix this once and for all?'
- ■ 'If I have to deal with this again, I'll scream!'
- ■ 'I thought my predecessor dealt with this.'

When the Cure is Worse than the Disease

Sometimes the short-term fix not only fails to solve the problem but it also makes it worse *and* makes it more difficult to solve the fundamental difficulty. Then the system has to rely on the fix to keep going. What begins as a temporary repair insinuates itself until it is an essential part of the system, just like an addictive drug. By creating the need for itself, it is hero and villain rolled into one.

For example, a late night coffee keeps you alert, but then sleep does not come easily. Climbing out of bed in the morning, you need a couple of cups of strong coffee to wake you up. A mid-morning coffee and cake keep you going, but you lose your appetite for lunch and need another coffee to get you over that post-prandial slump in the early afternoon. More coffee in the evening repeats the cycle. But without the coffee you feel worse in the short term.

At its worst, this is the story of addictions. An addiction is a short-term solution that you come to rely on. It weakens your fundamental ability to solve the problem and can grow to become a worse problem, because you usually need more and more to have the same effect. Cigarette smoking is one example. Smoking is relaxing, so perhaps a person takes up the habit while under stress at work. At first a cigarette does make them feel more at ease (once they get over the initial nausea), but nicotine is also a stimulant and highly addictive. Tranquillizers and anti-depressants are other examples of drugs that can be dangerous when relied on to remove the symptoms of stress if the causes of that stress are not also investigated. Alcohol is another way of 'drowning your sorrows', but the sorrows never stay drowned and the drink itself can become a far worse problem than the original sorrows, while doing nothing to alleviate them.

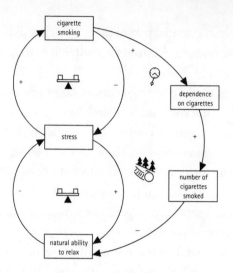

Addictions

In this system, the balancing loop is attempting to solve the problem, but the reinforcing loop makes it worse by reinforcing the habit while weakening the fundamental solution (the natural ability to relax), because nicotine is a stimulant. A further loop could be drawn to show how the number of cigarettes smoked can lead to health problems and more stress.

Some medical treatments may relieve symptoms but lead to worse problems. A iatrogenic illness is one caused by medical treatment. For example, steroid drugs are used to stop inflammation, but they also suppress the immune system and can lead to weight gain, fluid retention, depression, osteoporosis and headaches.

This story is easiest to see in chemical addictions, where the phrase 'quick fix' takes on a more sinister meaning, but it operates in other places too. It is possible to become addicted to all sorts of activities, if you come to rely on them to provide a quick answer and a way of avoiding the real question. Recently we have heard of addictions to the National Lottery, exercise, the

Internet and computer games. The system *structure* will be the same. Just replace 'cigarettes' with the relevant addiction.

The same system operates at a global level. A developing country may get substantial aid from other countries, and this can lead to a dependence on foreign aid and a weak internal economy. The weak economy makes it difficult to become more self-reliant and do without the foreign aid. To put it another way, 'Give a person a fish and you feed them for a day. Teach a person to fish and you feed them for a lifetime.' By giving them a fish you may also discourage them from fishing for themselves.

The same story operates whenever someone is too helpful, especially to children. We naturally want to help children, yet sometimes the best thing is to let them find their own way. We can see the same story playing out again when one person depends too much on another for a sense of self-esteem, security, even identity. The more they look to the other person, the less they are able to develop an independent sense of self-esteem and security for themselves. Whenever a person becomes necessary rather than simply available, this addictive systems story begins to creep in.

Businesses can become addicted to outside consultants to solve their problems rather than developing their own people. One business we know relied on regular motivational training to stimulate its sales force. As time went on, the staff relied more and more on this type of training; they became used to getting energy and ideas from the outside, rather than generating them for themselves in the business. We have seen training that cultivates dependence on the trainer even as it emphasizes self-reliance. This gives the mixed message, 'Rely on me to make you independent.'

Both individuals and businesses may become addicted to a form of crisis management. A person may not organize their work very well, so that tasks are always done in a atmosphere of nail-biting tension and rush. Once done, with a great sigh of relief, they are congratulated for saving the day and pulling out all the stops at the last minute. If they do not get much recognition normally, this can be very pleasant. But they may have left important tasks undone to cope with the crisis. Then these in turn become urgent and there is more pressure. Heroic efforts to deal with these essentially self-created crises may become the normal way of doing business. The company may then institutionalize and encourage this crisis-management style by giving rewards for efforts above and beyond the call of duty, not seeing that the very rewards reinforce the crises and that there is a fundamental flaw in the system that is creating constant last-minute panics.

Here are some phrases that strongly suggest this pattern is present:

- 'Just once more won't do any harm...'
- 'The next time this happens we really will look at it afresh.'
- 'When this emergency is over, we will return to our normal standards.'
- 'I don't want to keep doing this but somehow I can't help it...'
- 'I'll give up tomorrow...'
- 'I wish we could stop this, it's not doing any good.'
- 'I know it doesn't help in the long run, but what else can we do?'

There are three clues that let you know you are caught up in this story. First you feel helpless, swept along by events. Second, the problem gets worse as time goes by, and third, you become weaker and less able to solve the fundamental problem.

Where are the leverage points? Look at the way you are currently solving the problem. What are the alternatives? This is a story where the 'solution' is the most pressing problem, so anything that weakens the first balancing loop with its problem 'solution' the better. At the same time there is a fundamental problem, so anything that strengthens the other balancing loop that contains the fundamental solution is useful.

Think out the side-effects of the symptomatic solution. What other ways are there to solve the problem that would not have these side-effects? This story may have built up over a long time and it may take time to completely resolve it.

We have been talking about finding a 'fundamental solution' but is there ever such a thing? All solutions have side-effects. The most important question is whether these effects add to the health and well-being of the system or detract from it. And what is a fundamental solution on one level may be less good when viewed from another perspective. One person's gain may be another's loss. Once again, we are faced with the puzzle of 'turtles all the way down'. Is the fundamental solution the place where the turtles stop?

Maybe the process of exploring, questioning and finding answers at many levels is more important than chasing that elusive final turtle. After all, solutions only work on certain levels. Perhaps the most important question to ask is whether your solution fits into the ethics, values and identity of the system. If you are that system, then systems thinking challenges you to think about those. If the business is the system, then it is important that it has a vision, mission and set of core values that are fully known and lived. If your body is that system, then you need to have a experiential knowledge that comes from listening to what your body is telling you. Sometimes the leverage is in questioning your standards. And at other times, it can be vitally important that you are true to those standards.

Life is Like a Poker Game

Have you ever been in a situation where you feel threatened, so you decide to give as good as you get, but then you find yourself pushed into a corner and you can't back down without loss of face? Yet you can't go on, for the price has got too high. It's a poker game where you want to stay in the game, but your money is running out fast.

This is the story of the arms race, the price war and the stand-off fight. In a price war, company A (let's call them Asbury's) starts selling at a discount. Company B (let's call them Tescway), becomes nervous that they will lose their market share and drops their price. Asbury's responds by a further reduction and Tescway, not to be outdone, follows suit. Both companies may end up losing money, but neither may back down because they would lose custom to the other who might then make a profit through benefits of scale from the extra customers. Both parties see the other's actions as a threat and both respond by doing the same.

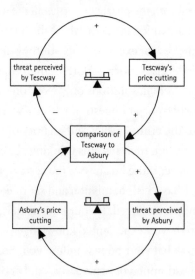

Escalation

In this system, two balancing loops add up to a growing conflict. When confronted with this pattern, you have three leverage points. First, the mental models behind the conflict. For this system to operate, both sides have to share two ideas. First, that they are playing for fixed resources. Second, that they are playing a zero sum game. In other words one company's loss is the other's gain. Life, in other words, appears to be a poker game. Without this shared mental model, the companies' actions do not make sense. Both sides also have to stick blindly to their own point of view. Each has to see their own behaviour as defensive and the other's behaviour as aggressive. Eventually this logic leads countries to attack others to defend themselves. If they were to step outside and see the system and how they are interacting from the outside, the scales would fall from their eyes.

Is one side's gain truly another's loss?

Are the resources really fixed or are they expandable?

It takes two to have a price war or an arms race, so unilateral action can break the spiral. A zero sum game can only flourish in an atmosphere of secrecy and mutual distrust. When Gorbachev ended the arms race with America in the 1980s, he acted on the idea that the Soviets could get *more* security if they had *fewer* weapons, so he made unilateral arms cuts. He had to do this publicly. Doing it in secret would not have had the same effect. Such a move is a public communication to the other party that you have some degree of trust and that you are not willing to play the game any more.

The second leverage point is the nature of the comparison. Are the two sides comparing the same thing? They think they are, but only from their own limited point of view. It may be possible to reframe the goal as Gorbachev did. Even a poker player throws in the occasional hand in order to come out ahead at the end of the evening.

Thirdly, it may be possible to move up a level and ask what larger goal would include both parties' goals. The question to ask is: *What does that goal get for them?* When you know that, it may be possible to find another way of satisfying that higher level goal.

Suspect this escalation pattern is present when you hear these sorts of phrases:

- 'I've got to match them step for step.'
- 'If only they would let up then we could too.'
- 'I'm not letting this go without a fight.'
- 'If they think they can get away with that they have another think coming.'
- 'It's too late to pull out.'
- 'I'll not be the first to back down.'
- 'I'm with you every step of the way.'

The Monopoly Pattern

Escalation is one response to competition. Another response is a slow, seemingly inevitable drift in favour of one side. This seems like a self-fulfilling prophecy in a competitive environment. Money attracts money and success begets success. One side may start with a slight edge and gets good results, which leads to more people investing in it at the expense of its competitor. The more it gets, the more it gets, which has led to this story being called 'success to the successful'. It is a pleasure indeed to be on the winning side of this story, but not so good to be on the losing side. If you have ever played *Monopoly*, then you will know this story well.

Competition between local schools in England is an excellent example. Schools receive money from their local education authority based on the number of children they attract. The more money they have, the more facilities they can provide and the more attractive they become to parents who want to send their children to a good school. Public examination results are published as country-wide 'league tables' and parents can see which schools are getting the best results, in an atmosphere that puts a lot of store on good examination results as a passport to a good job.

Imagine two hypothetical schools. Mount Ararat Secondary School is in a nice part of town and is doing well. It started with a good reputation and it is always oversubscribed, so is reasonably funded by the local education authority. Its examination results are good, parents want to send their children there, and the children, coming from homes that value educational achievement, are committed to doing well. The parents support the school, there is an active Parent Teacher's Association, and the parents are prepared to raise money for extra resources and educational trips outside school. With the extra resources and committed students, the school's examination results get better. The school becomes more attractive still and parents are prepared to move into the area to get the best schooling. The word gets round that Mount Ararat's is the school to go to if you want a good education – it must be because it is so popular and oversubscribed. It also attracts good teachers, who enhance its success.

St Spiral's Secondary School, on the other hand, is in a slightly poorer part of the borough. Its academic results were not quite so good at the beginning, and with the more affluent and committed students going to Mount Ararat, they slip still further. Over the years, they may continue to slide, leading to low morale, high staff turnover and discipline problems among the children.

This structure is the monopoly pattern or the 'success to the successful' archetype.

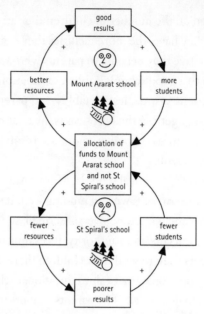

The monopoly pattern

Balance between work and family time is another example.
The more time you devote to work, the more successful you
may be, but this may be at the expense of your family. This
creates tension, perhaps arguments when you are at home,
making home even less attractive, and more and more of your
time and creative energy may be put into your work. In this
example, there may be a drifting goals pattern at work too. You
may fully intend to spend more time with your family but somehow something important always seems to come up at the last
minute... If you find yourself in the grip of this pattern, the
leverage points are to watch for drifting goals, be clear about
your own values in work and family, and to take an outside view,
to see the system. When you see it from the outside, you are
no longer caught in it.

Where are the other leverage points? In the school system there are many. The excellence of the staff, overall morale of the school and the leadership skills of the head teacher, for example, can all make a big difference in counteracting the pattern.

The monopoly pattern presupposes competition. And, like escalation, it assumes that there are scarce resources and that it is a zero sum game – one side's loss is the other side's gain. This insight leads to some questions:

■ Is the competition really necessary?
■ What is the larger goal that both sides are trying to achieve?
■ What are the scarce resources at stake?
■ Are they really limited?
■ Would co-operation serve all parties better?

This story often plays out in business where a number of junior managers are coached for a few senior positions or the same problem is given to several different teams. But why waste resources? If you want one winner, it might be better to identify what is important to success and teach it. That would improve results for everyone.

When you look at the monopoly pattern from another point of view, it actually uses resources in a way that creates a loser or a failure. What a waste. In business it makes sense to create an environment and values where everyone can give their best in the service of a more encompassing goal.

The system pattern also depends on the resources necessary to achieve good results being used as rewards – for the very results they are meant to help achieve. It rewards the winners with the means to win again. Such resources may be better allocated by need than by result.

The success to the successful pattern is especially frustrating and unjust if it penalizes the losers at the same time. When social rewards follow this systems pattern it leads to injustice, anger and indignation. This story has deep social implications. The winners in this system are not going to change the system that made them winners. Taken to its limit, this pattern can destroy democracy.

It is interesting that there are many rules in competitive sports that discourage or interrupt this system pattern. The reason is obvious: in the end it destroys the game. No one wants to play a game where the end is predetermined from the start. It is no fun, not even for the winners. Alternating the serve, tossing coins for first use of the ball, switching sides so the sun is not always in your eyes, home and away games, and handicaps are all devices used in sport to limit the system pattern.

These phrases indicate that the monopoly pattern may be operating:

- 'They are doing so well, they deserve more funding.'
- 'The rats are jumping a sinking ship.'
- 'This will help them build on their success.'
- 'What is up for one is down for another.'
- 'There have to be winners and losers, that's life.'
- 'It wasn't a level playing field...'
- 'That's kicking them when they are down...'
- 'They are getting all the breaks.'

The Tragedy of the Commons

The last story is a tragedy. Like all dramatic tragedies, everyone acts in what seems like their own best interests, yet the consequences are calamitous. Everyone can act reasonably, with perfect sense, and the result can be a perfect *non*sense.[3]

Joseph lives close to an adventure theme park and one hot day last summer, he and his family decided to spend a day there. Unfortunately, so did everyone else in the country, or so it seemed. The car park was full to bursting, the rides had long queues, the swimming pool had so many people in it that you could not swim two strokes without colliding with another swimmer. The restaurants had huge queues and many of them were running out of supplies by lunchtime. The weather was perfect, the rides were good, it could have been a perfect day out ... for half the people. Joseph was surely not the only one wishing that fewer people had come to the park.

This story is very common. You can see it in action on a large scale with holiday resorts – beautiful unspoilt beaches are discovered and as more and more people flock to them, they lose the unspoilt charm that attracted people in the first place. You can see it world-wide with the Internet – while new web pages are appearing at a rate of thousands a day, the speed of access at peak times makes frozen treacle sliding down an igloo wall look hurried.

At a critical threshold, there is no more slack in the system and every new user brings down the benefit for everybody. What is a gain for an individual is a pain for the crowd. Stonehenge used to be open for all to wander round freely and touch. Now, everyone has to admire it from afar, because the constant movement was undermining the stones and the constant touching was starting to wear them away. Every year the problem becomes more acute for Britain's National Parks. For example, the Peak District park is the second busiest in the world, taking over 30 million visitors a year. Only Japan's Mount Fuji park takes more. Summer bank holidays are notorious for the long traffic jams that bring gridlock to large parts of beautiful countryside. Angry

drawing conclusions

motorists have ample opportunity to see the sights – but from their car windows as they crawl along.

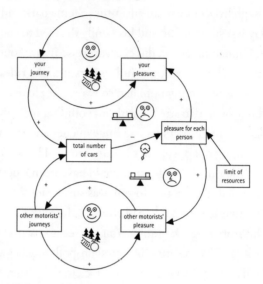

The tragedy of the commons

This system structure is known as the tragedy of the commons. In the first reinforcing loop at the top, your journey gives you pleasure, so you want to make more journeys. And you are not alone – the same reinforcing loop at the bottom applies to everyone else who wants to appreciate the beauty of the countryside. The total number of cars and the pleasure for each person form a balancing loop for you and everyone else. After a while nobody gains and everybody may lose, because there is a limit to the resources. This limit is set outside and independent of the system. The tragedy operates as use breaches the limits and the people within the system act as if it is not there.

This pattern will be present whenever you see a resource overused, with more and more people getting less and less individual benefit. Here are some giveaway phrases:

'This used to be so good, but now everyone knows about it.'
'I wish we could go back to when only few people knew of this.'
'In the good old days...'
■ 'I can't get my share, the pie's not big enough.'
'If I stop, what good will it do? Everyone else will just carry on. I'll be the only one to lose.'
'It used to be so good.'
'What are all these people doing?'
'Everybody's jumping on the bandwagon.'

You cannot solve the tragedy of the commons at an individual level. *All* the people involved will usually want to carry on using the resource while restricting others' right to do so. Finding the leverage must involve taking a systems perspective over the whole picture, otherwise the resource may become exhausted and nobody will benefit.

First you have to identify the commons:

What exactly is the common resource?
What are the limits?
■ Can the common resource be replenished or renewed?
What are the incentives for individuals to use the commons?
Who (if anyone) controls the incentives?
Can the commons be administered for a common good?
How long is the time horizon for damage to the commons?
How can everyone be educated about the total effect of their actions?

To go back to National Parks, they are using a combination of parking restrictions, speed limits, entrance fees, closed-off roads and internal public transport systems to improve the area for the visitors. Some of these schemes meet opposition from local residents. For example, in 1996, North Yorkshire Moors National Park wanted to introduce a car park at a nearby village which would operate on the principle of the longer you stay, the less you pay. They would then provide a network of buses into the park attractions. Local traders were worried about the effect on their business if short-term shoppers were put off and threatened to open fields for free parking, so the scheme was dropped. The proposed solution met a balancing loop limit in the perceptions of the local businesses.

One mental model to question is whether we need the use of our private cars in a National Park. For many holidays, we take it for granted that we will not have the use of a car. Many National Parks do ban private cars altogether. This works, providing there is good public transport.

The tragedy of the commons is the last of the main system stories, the archetypes, that we will consider. You may meet it again, or some other familiar patterns, when you start to draw your own stories. Remember, drawing systems' stories is visual, starts from your real experience and reflects fundamental events. It gives a real structure to your intuitions and is creative problem solving at its most effective.

---

1 Daly, Herman, 'Towards some operational principles of sustainable development', *Ecological Economics* 2 (1990), 1–6

2 *British Medical Journal* 310, 18 March 1995, 750

3 This pattern was first put forward by the ecologist Garrett Hardin. *See* Hardin, Garrett, 'The tragedy of the commons', *Science*, 13 December 1968

Drawing Conclusions

PROBLEM SOLVING WITH SYSTEMS PATTERNS

■ Building successful performance.
Reinforcing loop.

■ Growth slows, there is less and less result for the same effort.
Limits to success – the reinforcing loop has met a balancing loop.

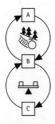

■ Continuous effort but little improvement from the beginning.
Goals drifting upwards or set too high.

■ Continuously slipping performance.
Goals drifting downwards.

■ You are forced to keep step with others to your disadvantage.
  Escalation.

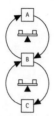

ACHIEVING A GOAL OR STANDARD WITH SYSTEMS THINKING

■ *Balancing loop.*

■ Continual overshooting and then underachieving.
  Balancing loop with delays.

■ Problem keeps returning.
  Short-term fix is not working.

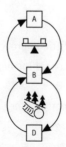

- **Problem gets worse.**

  More reliance on short-term solution.

  Overall performance goes down.

  Addiction, reinforcing side-effect is weakening fundamental solution.

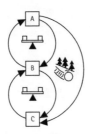

- **Seemingly inevitable drift towards whoever started best.**

  Success to the successful, the monopoly pattern.

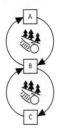

- **Everybody wants the same thing and is getting less and less of it.**

  Tragedy of the commons.

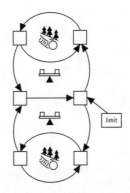

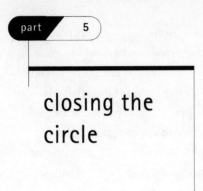

part 5

closing the circle

Here are some conclusions, recollections and signposts pointing back to where we have been and forward to where we can go. Systems thinking will be of help wherever you are, and just when life seems at its most unfair and a situation most intractable is when a systems structure may be operating. If you recognize a problem as an old friend, or even a party bore that you cannot shake off, there is almost certainly a systemic structure to the situation. To resolve it, you must first unravel it. This will extend your area of choice and control over what happens.

To expand your area of influence, look first to yourself. There is no influence without responsibility. Responsibility is often confused with blame. When someone says, 'Are *you* responsible for this?' it usually means you are in trouble. However, responsibility is not blame. It is the ability to respond. And the more choices you have, the better your ability to respond.

When you find yourself caught in any repetitive problem situation, start with the question, 'How am I maintaining this situation?' Feedback loops are circles and the only point of influence you have is where you and the loop come together. Then look to how your actions connect with other people and how the situation builds. Your behaviour may look like a response from your perspective but it may look like an unprovoked action from another perspective. When you look to yourself first, you reconnect yourself with your experience, so you complete the feedback circle.

When you start to think in systems, there is no blame, and no self-blame either. There is a widely shared mental model that if something goes wrong, it must be someone's fault. The buck, as they say, has to stop somewhere. But once you sense feedback loops, you will see the buck stops everywhere and nowhere. It goes round in a circle. No one person can be completely responsible in a system. What often happens is that everyone acts in what seems like their best interests from their perspective, but the total combination of feedback leads in another direction entirely. However, we are not helpless, we do have leverage and influence once we see the system.

What happens to us is feedback. It is the result in part of our own actions coming back at us, somewhere, sometime. Perhaps days, months or years ago we dropped a stone into a pool and now we feel the waves. Imagine many other people also dropping their stones into the pool. The pattern of ripples can be very complex, almost unrecognizable, and while you had a hand in it, so did many others. Blame becomes ridiculous, but we still have responsibility for our stone. We contribute to the total pattern.

When you are caught in a system pattern; for example, the tragedy of the commons, what happens to you is because of your position in the system. *It's not personal.* It's inevitable. It is part of the system you are in. Behaviour is mostly determined by the structure of the system. Change the system structure and you can change the results. But in order to change the system structure you have to understand the system.

Here are some guidelines.

Make Connections

Everything you experience is feedback. You had a hand in making it. This means that you need to think in circles rather than straight lines. You need to make the connection.

The prevailing paradigm derived from centuries of science tends to see cause – effect – stop. It splits the world and splits our experience. Therefore it divides us from the word and separates us from our experience and the consequences of our actions. Thinking in circles gives much more power and flexibility. There is more than one way to punctuate experience. When we think in feedback loops we connect back with our own experience, we are truly in the world. We are not out of touch, looking on from a distance, hearing echoes rather than voices.

Systems thinking connects you to your senses, because they are the only way you can get feedback. Seeing relationships, being a part of those relationships and thinking in circles is, we believe the most important part of systems thinking. This simple but profound shift in thinking will change your world from a set of static cause–effect relations, like some galactic bar billiard game, to an ongoing, dynamic, self-sustaining process where you are centre stage.

You Never Just Do One Thing

There are always side-effects. And what is a 'side-effect' from your perspective may be a very 'central effect' for someone else. So when the sales department of a business starts taking special orders, the side-effect may be pressure on manufacturing, and for manufacturing, this may be a serious problem. The question is whether the side-effects are serious enough to create balancing feedback to the originator of the loop. In this case, the manufacturing division might politely request the sales department to stop taking so many *special* orders. (Orders are fine, but specials cause problems.) Or manufacturing may have trouble producing them, leading to delays and consequent pressure on customer service. This would also be feedback, only here, manufacturing might be blamed.

While side-effects can cause problems, they also work in our favour in a very powerful way. For example, energy conservation would save us money in the household budget and also reduce air pollution, therefore reducing the number of respiratory diseases and asthma among children. This would reduce some of the burden on the National Health Service in treating these diseases, which might release money for other medical treatment in other areas. It would also cut acid rain, greenhouse gases and radioactive wastes. Such is the systemic nature of the modern economy that there is probably no area that would not feel an effect.

What stops us?

Results Are Not Proportional to Effort

You can get a big change for a small effort when you know the leverage point. Conversely, unless you understand the system, you can find yourself putting a lot of effort into trying to influence with no effect whatever. We have seen from the limits to success pattern that trying to push the reinforcing loop is a waste of time, when there is a counteracting balancing loop. Your own force is transformed round the balancing loop and used against you. The harder you push, it seems the harder the system pushes back, but the system only channels your own force. The answer is to weaken the balancing loop, to find out what stops the growth.

When you have a problem, systems thinking suggests some other useful questions to ask:

The first questions are:

■ What do I want?
■ What have I got?

In trying to achieve your goal, you have set up a balancing feedback loop, which is driven by the difference between what you have now and what you want. It is best to be explicit about both of these.

Secondly, you need to ask:

■ What stops this problem from being resolved?
■ How is this problem maintained?
■ What am I doing that is maintaining this problem?'

These questions will get you to the structure of the problem, without blame.

Thirdly, you need to look at the feedback you have:

■ What are my results so far?
■ What have I learned from them?

Lastly, look at the mental models you are holding about the problem:

■ What am I assuming about the problem?
■ What am I assuming about the people involved?'

With these questions you can begin to map the system.

Your mental models are part of the system you are trying to

understand, so when you draw your boundary round the system, make sure you include yourself inside it. As Gregory Bateson, one of the pioneers of system thinking in the 1950s, is reputed to have said, 'When the investigator starts to probe unknown areas of the universe, the back end of the probe is always driven up his own vital parts.'[2]

A System Works as Well as its Weakest Link

One way of changing a system is to look for the weakest link. The place where the system will break down when under pressure can be used as a leverage point to make the system more efficient or responsive. The speed of a journey depends on its slowest phase. If a journey takes an hour and 15 minutes of that is spent in a traffic jam at one junction, then by finding a way round that one place, you can increase your speed by 25 per cent.

Another example is a supplier filling a customer order. The order may be placed with the manufacturer smoothly and efficiently. The manufacturer may have an excellent inventory system, obtain the part very quickly and deliver it to the supplier. But then it could take a week to reach the customer because of delivery problems.

Here's a personal example. Some time ago Joseph bought a new keyboard for his computer. After a few days it developed a fault, so he telephoned the supplier and asked for a replacement under guarantee. Urgently. Three days passed. When he telephoned again, the supplier said the manufacturer wanted the old (new!) keyboard back before they could issue a replacement. Joseph, wishing that someone had told him this three days ago, sent it back by special courier. Three more days passed.

He telephoned again. The company had lost the receipt from the courier. Without the receipt, the keyboard did not officially exist and therefore could not be replaced. Joseph told them to find the receipt. That was their problem, not his. Eventually, after two weeks, he got the keyboard. The weak link was presumably the communication between the supplier and the manufacturer. You probably have some equally frustrating examples.

These sorts of delays happen much more often when the person who has to deal with the customer is not empowered to make a decision without consulting a higher manager. Empowerment, together with a flatter business structure, has improved many parts of business.

Continuous improvement may work if you direct your efforts towards continuously improving the weakest or slowest link in the chain and keep the total system in mind. At the back of the weak link there is usually an unquestioned mental model that dictates this is how the situation has to be. Changing the mental model that creates the weak link is the generative learning that prevents the problem from happening again.

Looking at the principle of the weakest link from another angle, it implies that a system does not work as well as its strongest link. In a system you can have too much of a good thing. We know from personal experience that too little of any nutrient is a problem, but so is too much. Too much of *anything* is harmful (even water can kill you if you have too much of it). Money may be the only exception (although even this is doubtful beyond a certain level – research with lottery winners found that a year after their win, their self-reported level of happiness and satisfaction with life was almost the same as before their win).[3]

Also, when you try to maximize one part of a system, the feedback works in such a way to put pressure on other parts of the system. It puts it out of balance. So, when you make one part of the system very fast or very efficient, the system *as a whole* may become less efficient. For example, if you overdevelop some muscles, this puts unequal strains on the tendons where they insert into the bone and may well lead to injuries. Muscle groups have to balance. Whether they are overdeveloped or not is a question for your whole body, not just the particular muscles. Arnold Schwarzenneger's biceps look fine on him, but would look ridiculous on Woody Allen.

A business example: we know a company that hired a consultant to streamline their accounts department. This he did. His recommendations led to the department becoming much more efficient. Unfortunately, this meant they needed more information from the marketing division, which could not supply them without a great deal more work. Marketing complained and the overall efficiency of the organization went down until a compromise could be reached. Neither the consultant nor the organization had looked at the wider implications of the change. Accounts blamed marketing, marketing blamed accounts, and they both blamed the consultant.

Good enough for each part is often best for the whole system.

There is another implication. It is the adaptable that do best in the long term, not the well adapted. When you make part of a system super-efficient or very fast, you are only making it so for that particular time and context. Times change. Contexts change. Therefore what is well adapted to one environment is not so well adapted to a new one. Every adaptation is bought at the price of some flexibility in the face of changing circumstances. The moment you are best adapted is the moment you are most vulnerable to change. Every solution creates new problems. When you are most successful is the time you should be actively researching your next step, next idea or next market. Don't try to change with the times – change *before* the times, or risk the times changing you.

Time Delays

We tend to think about the consequences of our actions in a linear way. We think of the action, then the possible consequences, then the consequences of those consequences, in a chain. We cannot see very far ahead, no more than the equivalent of a few moves in a chess game. We forget that there will be feedback in the system that will not appear until some time after. It may complete its circle much later and spoil our carefully thought out linear plan. We do not truly take time into account.

When we mentally rehearse, we rarely take in the time factor. In a way, all thought is a simulation – trying out possibilities and predicting the consequences inside the safety of your own brain, rather than jumping in and finding out the consequences for real. Real-life actions are irreversible – time does not flow backwards.

When we simulate, we build a model with sufficient detail to allow us to understand what we want to understand, look at the consequences and, if we do not like them, try something else to see if it turns out any better. Computer simulations are useful in building models of complex systems, for example management, ecology, urban planning, economics and, of course, the weather. There are many computer programs that can build sophisticated systems models and are easy to use. The computer can keep track of the many variables, feedback loops and time delays. The computer has no mental models, no hidden agenda and no wishful thinking. However, a computer simulation is no substitute for *understanding* and part of your understanding will be your own mental models. Computer simulation can be a useful test of our models, allowing us to refine them and then test them again in a reinforcing loop.

Systems thinking teaches us humility. We soon come to see that the world is more complex than any computer within it. Our conscious mind is not all knowing and all seeing, even with huge amounts of computing power. And we already know that rational behaviour for an individual can lead to disaster for the group – the tragedy of the commons archetype.

However, we can change the way we think, looking first at our part in the system, then at our mental models, taking time delays into account and realizing that we do not really escape the consequences of our actions. When we change the way we think, we will change the way we behave in a reinforcing loop, which in turn will change the way we think... And this may lead us to wiser counsels. There will never be a point where we know everything about everything. But it is enough to know enough.

This has been a personal view of systems thinking, part of a world-wide step forward in exploring practical and philosophical implications of systems concepts. We have more and more information, and the challenge is to see the connections, to have a system of knowledge and not a heap of facts. To know what is worth knowing. We hope this book is both practically useful and a contribution to this exploration of systems ideas. In a world where we have increasing power through technology and industry to reshape the Earth, we need the wisdom that comes from a broader vision.

Finally, in the words of Lao Tse, the author of the *Tao Te Ching*, that great systems treatise written 2,500 years ago:

When times are quiet it is easy to take action; ere coming troubles have cast their shadows, it is easy to lay plans. That which is brittle is easily broken, that which is minute is easily dissipated. Take precautions before the evil appears, regulate things before disorder has begun. The greatest tree sprang from the tiniest shoot. The tallest tower rose from a little mound of earth. A journey of a thousand miles began with a single step. A great principle cannot be divided, therefore many containers cannot contain it.

1 Our thanks to Rick Karash for his ideas in developing this approach. *See* 'Going deeper', *The Systems Thinker* 6, 9, November 1995

2 Lipset, D., *Gregory Bateson: The legacy of a scientist*, Prentice-Hall, 1980

3 Brickman, P., 'Adaptation level determinants of satisfaction with equal and unequal income distributions in skill and change situations', *Journal of Personality and Social Psychology* 32 (1975), 191–8

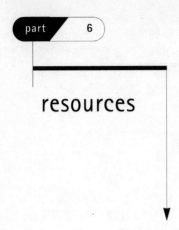

part 6

resources

a brief history of systems thinking

Some ideas seem so obvious it takes time for them to reveal their deeper implications and catch people's interest. It proves the old adage that if you want to conceal a secret, put it in plain sight and everyone will assume it is mundane. Man certainly had a working knowledge of gravity before Sir Isaac Newton was struck by the infamous apple, but it was Newton who opened up the science of physics and started us on the long road from the fall of an apple to the hum of particle acceleration chambers. Once he had developed the concept of gravity, what had been a fact of life became a concept, a principle and a step towards greater understanding of the universe. It could be used and built on. Now, with some help from Einstein, gravity underpins our physics and cosmology, even our ideas of how the universe may have started and where it might end.

Thomas Kuhn, the eminent scientific historian, wrote about 'paradigm shifts' in his book *The Structure of Scientific Revolutions* (University of Chicago Press, 1962). At any time, current theory forms a paradigm – a self-reinforcing mental model. Science only advances, Kuhn wrote, when we find interesting discrepancies between theory and practice. Once the first cracks appear, we are sensitized and search out these anomalies. More and more of them are brought to light until, like the Copernican celestial wheels that at one time 'explained'

the orbits of the planets, the current paradigm becomes so con-
voluted in trying to explain these annoying facts that the whole
structure collapses under the weight of its own incoherence.
A new theory then arises from the ashes of the old, or the old
is modified in significant ways.

Maybe, there is another way that paradigms can change.
What if facts that have hitherto been taken for granted are ques-
tioned until something new and interesting emerges? Nature,
for instance, builds systems naturally (of course). She doesn't
build anything else. But these systems are certainly not neat and
orderly. Living systems are uncontrollable, unpredictable, but
very adaptable. The complex systems within them are not easy
to imitate or unravel. Perhaps we have been too immersed in
natural systems to be able to study them in an objective way.

Pragmatism fuels the advance of knowledge. Systems
thinking advanced as people figured out ways to make a useful
difference.

If we trace the development of systems thinking as man's ability
to appreciate and put the systemic principles of feedback, emergence and circuitous thought into practice, then the first system,
at least the first we know of, was invented by a man named
Ktesibios, who lived in Alexandria in the third century BC. He is
credited with many inventions, among them a water clock with a
self-regulating water supply. A constant flow of water at a regular
speed drove the mechanism. The water flowed over a floating
cone-shaped regulating valve. As the water level increased, this
cone was pushed upwards into the funnel that let in the water and

partially blocked it. This diminished the flow and lowered the level, the valve dropped and more water was let in. The valve soon found a position which let in just enough water to hold it there. Without such a valve, the water flow would decrease, there would be less pressure and the clock would slow down. Non-regulating clocks had to be replenished by hand. Ktesibios's clock worked. So the ancestor of our modern carburettor floating valve was invented over 2,000 years ago to tell the time.

A century later a man named Heron, also from Alexandria, built on Ktesibios's work and made several float valves based on the same principle. It was not until the eighteenth century that any mechanical feedback system was built that was not based on one of Heron's prototypes, apart from a primitive thermostat invented by a Dutch alchemist named Drebbel about 1605. He needed a constant temperature in his furnace to transmute lead into gold and built a thermostat which worked on exactly the same principles as the thermostats we now have in our homes. His thermostat worked, but his experiment was unsuccessful. If only he had known, he could have made his fortune by patenting the thermostat instead! However, he never published his design and the thermostat was not rediscovered for another 100 years.

Turning to medicine and physiology, perhaps the next major step forward was by the English physician William Harvey, who discovered the circulation of the blood. He published his ideas in 1628, showing how the heart pumped the blood round the body and finally refuting the prevailing theory, dating back to Galen in 170, that the liver was the central organ of the blood system and moved the blood to the edge of the body to form flesh. The heart and blood vessels are indeed a system, and they make a circle. The continuous change and movement of the heart and blood from moment to moment keep our internal environment steady. Medicine has slowly unravelled many of our bodily systems since then, not only showing how each is a homeostatic system, that is, it regulates itself, but also how the various systems all fit together for the whole to work. Now, with the new science of psychoneuroimmunology that has developed since the mid-1970s, we are discovering how body and mind work together as a larger system, how stress and emotional trauma can leave us susceptible to disease, how thoughts affect us physiologically in the form of neurotransmitters and how actions of drugs are dependent on our belief in them, as shown by the placebo effect.

The next instalment in the story of man-made systems came with James Watt. Born in 1736, he increased the power of the existing steam engines in two ways. First, he designed a separate condensing chamber, which prevented loss of steam in the cylinder. Secondly, and more importantly from our point of view, in 1788 he invented the centrifugal governor, a revolutionary feedback device that automatically regulated the speed of the engine, for by adjusting the governor, the driver could control the engine to a steady rate.

The governor consisted of two lead balls that swung from a small pole. The influx of steam caused the pole to rotate and the balls to spin. The faster the spin, the higher and faster the balls rotated, like a fairground carousel. They were linked to a valve on the pole which adjusted the amount of steam and so controlled the speed of the spinning pole. The higher the balls spun, the more they closed the valve and reduced the speed. This allowed a much greater degree of control than had been possible in the past.

Feedback circuits meant that machine power could be controlled and this accelerated the spread of the industrial revolution. Feedback allows self-regulation. A machine that uses feedback uses its own output to regulate its input – that is the basic concept of automation. 'Auto' means self, so an automatic device is something that powers itself. Anything that works 'automatically' uses feedback.

In 1948 Norbert Wiener, a professor of mathematics at the Massachusetts Institute of Technology (MIT), published a profoundly influential book called *Cybernetics* (MIT Press, 1948). The word 'cybernetics' comes from the Greek word *kybernetes*, meaning a steersman, a pilot who steers a boat. The word 'governor' comes from the same root. Wiener defined cybernetics as 'the science of communication and control in animal and machine'. It has made a major contribution to the study of systems. Cybernetics focuses on how a system functions, regardless of what the system is – living, mechanical or social. It tantalizes us with an ambitious promise – to unite different disciplines by showing the same basic principles are at work in all of them. Wiener proposed the same general principles that controlled the thermostat may also be seen in economic systems, market regulation and political decision-making systems. Self-regulation of systems by feedback, defined by Wiener as 'a method of controlling a system by reinserting into it the results of past performance', became an engineering principle and was taken up by nearly all aspects of technology. If you can fully control one variable in a process, you can indirectly control them all by building in feedback links. Servomechanisms developed as one application of this principle. They are a type of self-regulating machine where a controlling output signal is compared with a controlling input signal, and the difference is used to control the next output. Servomechanisms are particularly used in steering devices, such as on cars, and automatic pilots on ships, aircraft, missiles and space vehicles.

Cybernetics had been pre-empted in all but name, however, six years earlier. A number of innovative thinkers in biology, computer science, anthropology, engineering and philosophy had been meeting since 1942 in a series of conferences organized through the Josiah Macy Foundation. These famous Macy conferences were held every year from 1942 until 1951. Norbert Wiener took part. Other participants were Margaret Mead, the anthropologist; Gregory Bateson, who made wide-ranging contributions to the philosophy of science, psychiatry, evolutionary theory and systems thinking; John von Neumann, one of the founders of computer science; and Warren McCulloch, a pioneer in the field of artificial intelligence. Cybernetics and artificial intelligence, feedback control in social systems, humans and machines, and political game theory were all thrown into this heady intellectual brew. The interdisciplinary speculations in the Macy conferences (well chronicled in the book *The Cybernetics Group* by Steven Heims (MIT Press, 1991)), pushed back the boundaries of systems thinking and cybernetics. These have developed in many directions since then.

One development, also built on the idea that complex systems share certain organizing principles and these can be uncovered and modelled mathematically, was general systems theory. This came mainly from the work of the biologist Ludwig von Bertalanffy and was outlined in his book *General Systems Theory* (Braziller, 1968). General systems theory focuses on system structure, rather than system function, and is applied to complex systems in physics, chemistry, biology, electronics and sociology. It has also diversified into information theory and the construction of mathematical models of electrical circuits and other systems.

Systems analysis is a similar group of ideas dealing with decision-making to control and optimize social and technological systems. Karl Deutsch analysed the political process from a cybernetic viewpoint in his book *The Nerves of Government*, published in 1963.

In 1961, Jay Forrester applied the cybernetic principles to the problems of economic systems, urban industry and housing in his influential book *Industrial Dynamics* (Productivity Press, 1961). Forrester's work later broadened to include the study of other social and economic systems using computer simulation techniques, and is known as the field of system dynamics. Forrester used a computer model in his book *Urban Dynamics* (Productivity Press, 1969) to try to understand the causes of urban growth and decay. If it is possible to model the complex interplay of forces in cities, then perhaps the principles could be extended even further. It was this possibility that led the Club of Rome to sponsor a conference in 1970 on 'The Predicament of Mankind'. Forrester and his colleagues began to design a world system dynamics model that was rather like a global spreadsheet. The result was the hugely influential book *The Limits of Growth* (Signet, 1972) by Donella Meadows and colleagues. The book looked at possible relationships between pollution, population and economic growth, and used a computer model to draw conclusions about a sustainable future, which were (and still are) highly controversial. Their basic thesis is if present growth in world population, pollution, food production and use of natural resources goes unchecked, the limits to growth of the Earth will be reached within 100 years. Its sequel, *Beyond the Limits* (Earthscan Publications, 1992) took the analysis further and offered slightly more hopeful conclusions than the original text.

From the 1960s a new branch of cybernetics developed that focused on the relationship between the observer and the system they were studying. Known as second order cybernetics, it comes mainly from the work of Heinz von Foerster, and explores how people construct models of the systems in which they interact, on the premise that observers cannot be separated from the systems they are describing, and so there must be feedback between observer and system, as well as within the system being studied. Second order cybernetics has been influential in family therapy and the analysis of social systems, as well as having implications for the sciences of psychology and epistemology (how we know what we know). Francisco Varela and Umberto Maturana are two writers who have developed second order cybernetics through their books and research.

Systems thinking has broadened into many areas. It is in the writings of influential people like Stephen Hawking on physics and cosmology, Richard Dawkins in evolutionary biology and Deepak Chopra on medicine. Peter Senge brought systems thinking to the forefront of management and leadership with his influential book *The Fifth Discipline* (Doubleday, 1990), which also applied systems archetypes to business problems.

We hope this very brief and personal overview gives you an idea of the main steps in the development in systems thinking. Our hope is that systems and cybernetic ideas, having made such an incredible difference to our material lives, will now start to make a difference to our mental lives as well.

In Lewis Carroll's *Alice Through the Looking Glass*, the Red
Queen told Alice she had to run on the spot just to stay in the
same place. But you can never stay in the same place. Unless
you are moving and evolving, you are falling back. New ideas
lead to new ideas in a reinforcing feedback loop. Answers to our
questions are not the end of our quest but the beginning of a
new one, based on new, better questions. Our hope is that by
taking basic systems ideas and applying them to our everyday
life, we can find new ways of thinking, revitalize our ideas in
the present and build a future that draws us on, even as we
begin to realize it now.

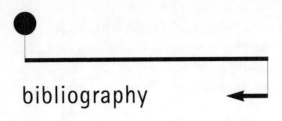

bibliography

Here is a personal selection of books. Some are classics of systems writing, others may become so. In the general section there are books we have enjoyed that use systemic thinking to illuminate their subjects.

Systems

Ashby, Ross, *Design for a Brain*, John Wiley, 1952

Bateson, Gregory, *Steps to an Ecology of Mind*, Ballantine, 1972

–, *Mind and Nature*, Bantam, 1972

Beer, Stafford, *Platform for Change*, John Wiley, 1975

Boulding, Kenneth E., *The World as a Total System*, Sage Publications, 1985

Checkland, Peter, *Systems Theory, Systems Practice*, John Wiley, 1981

Churchman, C., *The Systems Approach and its Enemies*, Basic Books, 1979

Forrester, Jay, *Industrial Dynamics*, Productivity Press, 1961

–, *Urban Dynamics*, Productivity Press, 1969

–, *Principles of Systems*, Productivity Press, 1990

Goodman, Michael, *Study Notes in System Dynamics*, MIT Press, 1974

Kauffman, Stuart, *The Origins of Order: Self-organization*, OUP, 1993

–, *Organization and Complexity*, Oxford University Press, 1995

Kosco, B., *Fuzzy Logic*, Flamingo, 1993

Meadows, Donella, and Meadows, Dennis, *The Limits of Growth*, Signet, 1972

Meadows, Donella, Meadows, Dennis, and Randers, Jorgen, *Beyond the Limits*, Earthscan Publications, 1992

Roberts, Nancy, *et al.*, *Introduction to Computer Simulation* Productivity Press, 1983

Scott-Morgan, Peter, *The Accelerating Organization*, McGraw-Hill, 1997

Senge, Peter, *The Fifth Discipline*, Doubleday, 1990

Senge, Peter, *et al.*, *The Fifth Discipline Fieldbook*, Doubleday, 1994

von Bertalanffy, Ludwig, *General Systems Theory*, Braziller, 1968

–, *Perspectives on General Systems Theory*, Braziller, 1975

Wheatley, Margaret J., *Leadership and the New Science*, Brett-Koehler, 1992

Cybernetics

Brand, Stewart, *Cybernetic Frontiers*, Random House, 1974

Keeney, Bradford, *Aesthetics of Change*, Guildford Press, 1983

Varela, Francisco, Thompson, Evan, and Rosch, Elanor, *The Embodied Mind*, MIT Press, 1993

von Foerster, Heinz (ed.), *Cybernetics of Cybernetics*, Gordon & Breach, 1979

Weinberg, Gerald, and Weinberg, Daniella, *General Principles of System Design*, Dorset House, 1979

Wiener, Norbert, *Cybernetics*, MIT Press, 1948

General

Capra, Fritjof, *The Turning Point: Science, society and the rising culture*, Simon & Schuster, 1982

Carse, James, *Finite and Infinite Games*, Penguin, 1986

Csikszentmihalyi, Mihaly, *The Evolving Self*, HarperCollins 1993

Dawkins, Richard, *The Blind Watchmaker*, W. W. Norton, 1987

Gilovich, Thomas, *How We Know What Isn't So*, Macmillan, 1991

Gleick, James, *Chaos: Making of a new science*, Viking, 1987

Kelly, Kevin, *Out of Control*, Fourth Estate, 1994

Kuhn, Thomas S., *The Structure of Scientific Revolutions*, University of Chicago Press, 1962

Lovelock, J., *Gaia: A new look at life on Earth*, Oxford University Press, 1979

Minsky, Marvin, *The Society of Mind*, Simon & Schuster, 1985

Morowitz, Harold J., *Cosmic Joy and Local Pain*, Charles Scribner & Sons, 1987

Prigogone, Ilya, *Order out of Chaos*, Bantam, 1984

Waldrop, M., *Complexity*, Simon & Schuster, 1993

Watzlawick, Paul, *Ultra-Solutions*, W. W. Norton, 1988

Wilber, Ken, *A Brief History of Everything*, Shambhala Publications, 1996

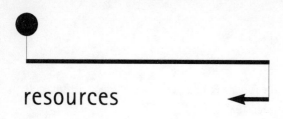

resources

Pegasus Communications Inc.

Pegasus publishes many excellent systems resources including *The Systems Thinker*, a monthly newsletter applying systems thinking to organizational practice. Pegasus also produces and distributes books, videotapes and audiotapes as well as introductory learning materials on systems thinking. They hold an annual conference – 'Systems Thinking in Action'.

Pegasus Communications Inc.
PO Box 120 Kendall Square
Cambridge, MA 02142–0001, USA
Tel: 617 576 1231
Fax: 617 576 3114

System Dynamics Review

John Wiley publish the quarterly journal of the System Dynamics Society, *System Dynamics Review*. Contact:

John Wiley & Son
Baffins Lane, Chichester
West Sussex, PO19 1UD

Tel: +44 01243 779777
Fax: +44 01243 775878

The Creative Learning Exchange (CLE)

The CLE publish excellent introductory materials on systems thinking and system dynamics from the System Dynamics in Education Project (SDEP). This is a self-teaching guide to the field of system dynamics assembled at MIT under the direction of Jay Forrester. You can obtain resources as written material, or on disk for the Apple Macintosh or PC. You can also obtain them from the CLE web site: http//:sysdyn.mit.edu

Creative Learning Exchange
1 Keefe Road
Acton, MA 01720
USA
Tel: 508 287 0070
Fax: 508 287 0080

Internet Resources

There are many newsgroups, World Wide Web sites and mailing lists about systems thinking. Here are some we think are particularly useful now. No doubt these will change and develop and more will be added. You can explore many other links from these sites.

WORLD WIDE WEB SITES

The Systemic University of the Net (SUN)

An excellent site with many links and learning resources about systems thinking: http://www.radix.net/crbnblu/

System Dynamics In Education Project (SDEP)

MIT site of systems learning materials under the direction of Jay Forrester: http//:sysdyn.mit.edu

The Principia Cybernetica Project (PCP)

A huge site on cybernetics and systems theory – a collaborative attempt to build a complete cybernetic philosophy. There are links to many other related subjects such as self-organization, artificial intelligence, language, evolution, political systems, ethics and the future development of systems: http://pesmc1.vub.ac.be

Practical Systems Thinking

Systems thinking and personal development – links, exercises and practical applications: http://www.lambent.com

Whole Systems

Part of the new Civilization network devoted to understanding whole systems: http://newciv.org/worldtrans/whole.html

MAILING LISTS

Cybsys-L

A mailing list devoted to systems science and cybernetics.
List address: cybsys-l@bingvmb.cc.binghampton.edu
Subscription address: listserv@bingvmb.cc.binghampton.edu

Cybernetics Discussion Group

List address: cybcom@gwuvm.gwu.com
Subscription address: listserv@gwuvm.gwu.com

Learning Organization List

Applying systemic thinking to business.
List address: learning-org-approval@world.std.com
Subscription address: majordomo@world.std.com

NEWSGROUPS

sci.systems

Discussion of the theory and application of systems science

Computer Systems Modelling Software

iThink (for Macintosh and PC)
Stella (for Macintosh and PC)

High Performance Systems
45 Lyme Road
Hanover, NH 03755, USA
Tel: 800 332 1202
Fax: 603 643 9502
Website: http://www.hps-inc.com/

Powersim (for PC)

Powersim AS
Postboks 206
5100 Isdalsto
Norway
Tel: +47 56 34 24 00
Fax: +47 56 34 24 01

Professional Dynamo (for PC)

41 William Limskey Way
Cambridge, MA 02172
USA
Tel: 617 864 8880
Fax: 617 864 8884

Microworlds (for Macintosh)

Microworlds Inc.
Kendall Square
PO Box 1400
Cambridge, MA 02142
USA
Tel: 617 225 0025
Fax: 617 225 0028

Vensim (for Macintosh and PC)

Vensim Product Centre
Ventana Systems Inc.
149 Waverley Road
Belmont, MA 02178
USA
Tel: 617 489 5249
Fax: 617 489 5316
Website: http://www.std.com/vensim

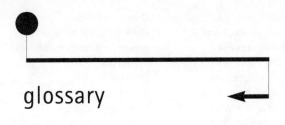

glossary

A

Addiction
The reliance on a short-term solution that causes a worse problem than the one it is meant to solve. This short-term solution then becomes necessary and fundamentally weakens the system at the same time.

Additive link
See Causal link.

Analysis
Breaking a whole into its parts in order to gain knowledge.

Archetype
See Systems archetype.

Attractors
Stable states where the system will settle.

B

Boundary
The edge of a system as determined by the observer.

C

Causal links
The connections between elements in a causal loop diagram.
- *additive reinforcing link*
  A change in one element adds to the next element.
- *balancing link*
  The first element has an opposing or balancing influence on the second when an increase (decrease) in the first results in the second becoming smaller (larger) than it would have been if the first had not changed.
- *proportional balancing link*
  The two elements move in proportion to each other. When one decreases the other increases. When one increases the other decreases.
- *proportional reinforcing link*
  The two elements move in proportion to each other. When one increases the other increases. When one decreases the other decreases.

– reinforcing link
The first element has a reinforcing influence on the second when an increase (decrease) in the first results in the second becoming larger (smaller) than it would have been if the first had not changed.

– subtractive balancing link
A change in one element subtracts from the next element.

Causal loop diagrams
Drawings of a system to show the feedback loops between the elements of the system and how they are related.

Chaos theory
Dealing with complex systems where a small change in initial conditions may make a huge difference to the outcome, thus making it unpredictable. Also how very complex systems can be built from repeating a series of simple rules.

Complementary relationship
Participants behave differently, and what they do fits together and sustains the relationship.

Complexity
Having many different connected parts.

– apparent complexity
Complicated in appearance, but with simple patterns underneath.

– detail complexity
Having a large number of different parts.

– dynamic complexity
Having a great number of possible connections between the parts.

– inherent complexity
Multiple, simultaneous feedback loops, where small variations may make a large difference.

Construction
Creating something that is not there. One of the ways we build mental models.

Cybernetics
'The science of communications and control in animal and machine' (Norbert Wiener). It focuses on how a system functions regardless of what the system is – biological, social or mechanical.

D

Deletion
Selecting and filtering experience by blocking out some parts.

Distortion
Changing experience and reading different meanings into it.

Double bind
A situation where you have two choices, you want neither and you have to choose.

Drifting goals
A basic systems pattern where the goal of the system drifts up or down and threatens the

balance of the system. For example, ever-rising sales targets or falling customer service standards.

Dynamic equilibrium
Continually changing in order to stay balanced, like a tightrope walker who must move and sway to stay upright.

E

Emergent property
A property that only arises when the system is working, above and beyond the parts that comprise it.

Escalation
A system pattern where competition pushes two or more parties into more and more extreme positions that are ultimately against their own self-interest.

Experiences
Events we perceive through our senses.
- *one-sided*
  Where only one outcome is memorable.
- *two-sided*
  Where any outcome is memorable.

Exponential growth
Where the more a system grows, the more it can grow. It has a fixed doubling time. An example is compound interest on a bank account. Exponential growth is one possible result of reinforcing feedback.

F

Feedback
The output of a system re-entering as the input, or the return of information to influence the next step.
- *balancing feedback*
  Changes in the system feed back in such a way as to oppose the original change and so dampen the effect. Balancing feedback acts to reduce the difference between where a system is currently and its goal. It limits growth. (Sometimes called negative feedback.)
- *reinforcing feedback*
  Changes in the system feed back in such a way as to amplify the change, leading to more change in the same direction. Reinforcing feedback amplifies growth. (Sometimes called positive feedback.)

Feedback loop
A closed chain of cause and effect.

Feedforward
When the anticipated effect in the future, that has not yet happened, triggers its own cause.
- *balancing feedforward*
  Where the very prediction or anticipation of a change drives the system towards its predicted state – a self-fulfilling prophecy.
- *reinforcing feedforward*
  Where the very prediction or anticipation of a change drives the system away from its

predicted state – a self-defeating prophecy.

First position
Perceiving the world from one point of view only, being in touch with your own inner reality.

Fixes that fail
A systems pattern where attempts to solve a problem are short lived and the fundamental cause is unchanged. Consequently the problem keeps recurring.

Flow
A measurement of change over time, for example, birth rate, expenditure, usage of natural resources. Flows lead to a change in a level. (Also called a rate.)

Fractal
A pattern that is made up of itself – an iterated pattern.

G

General systems theory
Group of ideas and practices built on the principle that complex systems share certain organizing principles regardless of the content, and these can be uncovered and modelled mathematically.

Generalization
The process by which one experience comes to represent a whole class of experiences. One way of building mental models.

Goal
A desired state.

H

Homeostasis
Dynamic self-regulation. The condition of a system when it can maintain itself within acceptable limits in the face of unexpected disturbances.

I, J, K, L

Level
A quantity that accumulates over time, for example population, the number of people in a family or money in a bank account. (Also called a stock.)

Leverage
Being able to influence the system in the way you want for the least amount of effort.

Limits to success
A system pattern where performance initially goes up, but after a while reaches a limit and then slows or declines. (Also called limits to growth.)

M

Mental models
The ideas and beliefs we use to

guide our actions. We use them to explain cause and effect as we see them, and to give meaning to our experience.

Meta position
Taking a view outside the system you are in, so being part of a wider system.

Modal operators
A linguistic term for words that show rules and possibilities, for example 'should' and 'shouldn't', 'can' and 'cannot'.

Model
A simplified but practical description of how something works.

Modelling
Creating a model for the purposes of understanding. Often used to describe computer simulations of systems.

Monopoly pattern
See Success to the successful.

Multiple description
Having different points of view of the same event.

N, O

Oscillation
Continuously moving past a fixed point, first on one side and then the other.

Outcome
See Goal.

Overshoot
When the system goes beyond its target, usually because the time delay between cause and effect has not been taken into account, so more action is taken than necessary.

P, Q

Perspective
Point of view.

Proportional links
See Causal links.

Punctuation
Where we decide to start the feedback loop and how we make sense of sequences of events based on our mental models.

Purpose
The goal of the system.

R

Rate
See Flow.

Recursion
Applying the same principle to itself at different levels like a spiral staircase – continual self-reference.

Regression
The tendency of events over time to change towards an average value, therefore making extreme values misleading as evidence for future action.

S

Second order cybernetics
A branch of cybernetics that
focuses on the relationship
between the observer and the
system they are studying.

Second position
Experiencing the point of view
of another person.

Self-reference
Where a statement or event
refers to itself, like this one.

Stock
See Level.

Structure
The way in which elements in
a system are organized.

Subtractive link
See Causal links.

Success to the successful
A systems pattern where there
is competition for a limited
resource. The more successful
competitor is rewarded with
the resources needed to become
still more successful. The less
successful competitor withers
from lack of these resources.

Symmetrical relationship
One in which the participants
match behaviour, responding in
the same way.

Synthesis
Building parts into wholes for
greater understanding.

System
An entity with a purpose, that
maintains its existence and functions as a whole through the
interaction of its parts.
– closed system
A system which in theory has no
interaction with its environment.
In practice, all systems are open
to some degree. The more
closed the system, the more the
energy runs down within it (the
Law of Entropy).
– open system
A system that interacts with its
environment, gaining resources
across the boundary. All living
systems are open systems.

System archetype
A widespread system structure
that can be seen in many different contexts.

System delay
The delay between the action
of a system and the feedback
returning to it. The delay
between cause and effect.

Systematic
In a planned way. (Not the
same as systemic.)

Systemic
Using systems ideas.

Systems dynamics
A field of systems study that
includes building computer simulations to understand complex
social systems.

Systems modelling
See Modelling.

Systems thinking
A way of thinking that focuses on the relationships between parts forming a connected whole for a purpose.

T

Tragedy of the commons
A system pattern where a shared resource is overused by individuals and so gives less and less benefit to all.

Z

Zero sum game
An interaction where one side's loss is assumed to be another side's gain.

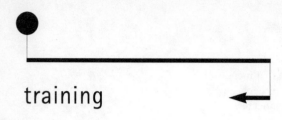

training

We have developed training in the art of system thinking.
These programmes are available as public seminars and also
designed in-house for business.

The training covers:

- how to think systemically
- the nature of feedback and how to work with it
- understanding and changing mental models
- understanding systems
- applying systems thinking to your personal and professional life
- developing systemic solutions

For details, contact:
  Lambent Training
  4 Coombe Gardens
  New Malden
  Surrey
  KT3 4AA
  Tel: +44 (0)181 715 2560
  Fax: +44 (0)181 715 2560
  Internet: www.lambent.com

or:

International Teaching Seminars
73 Brooke Road
London N16 7RD
Tel: +44 181 442 4133
Fax: +44 181 442 4155
Internet: www.nlp-community.com

CREDITS

We have done our best to track down and credit all the sources
for the material in this book. Please let us know by mail if we
have left out an important source or if someone is not properly
acknowledged. We will do our best to correct future printings.

FEEDBACK

Of course!
We want to learn from this book, so if you found it valuable and
would like to tell us why, or have any other responses or sugges-
tions, please let us know by post or e-mail.

index

Words marked * are in the glossary.

about the authors

Joseph O'Connor is a leading author, trainer and consultant in the field of communication skills, systems thinking and personal development. He is a certified trainer of Neuro-Linguistic Programming (NLP).

This book on the art of systems thinking has been a joy to write because it weaves together so many strands that have fascinated him for many years – how we learn, how we create our experience, and the deeper patterns that underlie seemingly unconnected events. It is a challenge and a pleasure to take these ideas and put them into a form that can be both interesting and practically useful.

Joseph works as a trainer and consultant in Europe, Asia and America. His clients include BT, UNIDO, Hewlett-Packard and ICI. He has written eight books (published in 13 languages), and is interested in most things under the sun.

Other books:

- *Introducing NLP* (with John Seymour)
- *NLP and Health* (with Ian McDermott)
- *Not Pulling Strings*
- *Practical NLP for Managers* (with Ian McDermott)
- *Principles of NLP* (with Ian McDermott)

- *Successful Selling with NLP* (with Robin Prior)
- *Training with NLP* (with John Seymour)

Videotapes:
- *Listening Skills in Music*

Audiotape:
- *An Introduction to NLP* (with Ian McDermott)

Contact Joseph at:

c/o Lambent Training
4 Coombe Gardens
New Malden
Surrey
KT3 4AA
Tel: +44 (0)181 715 2560
Fax: +44 (0)181 715 2560
E-mail: lambent@well.com
Website: www.lambent.com

Ian McDermott has been involved in change work with individuals and organizations for over 20 years. As director of training for International Teaching Seminars (ITS) he has been instrumental in demonstrating the practical applications of systemic thinking to thousands of people.

He has found that it is an approach that enables you to see the trees and the wood they are part of, to build new models and to think around limiting problems. However, as a consultant he has also found people frequently need help to implement this approach in real life situations. Hopefully this book will make systems thinking easier to use.

Ian is an internationally known author, trainer and consultant. Corporate clients include Coopers & Lybrand, BT, Prudential, Shell, J. Sainsbury and TSB. A certified trainer of Neuro-Linguistic Programming since 1988, Ian is also a registered UKCP psychotherapist. He was made an International NLP Diplomate in 1994 in recognition of his work in the field. Through his wife and two step-sons, Ian continues to learn about how systems work.

Other books:

Develop your Leadership Qualities (with Joseph O'Connor and others)
NLP and Health (with Joseph O'Connor)
Practical NLP for Managers (with Joseph O'Connor)
Principles of NLP (with Joseph O'Connor)
Take Control of your Life (with Joseph O'Connor and others)

Audiotapes:

An Introduction to NLP (Thorsons)
Deep Trance Relaxation (ITS)
Freedom from the Past (ITS)
Tools for Transformation (ITS)
What is NLP? (ITS)
Professional Development Program (ITS)

Contact Ian at:
    International Teaching Seminars
    73 Brooke Road
    London N16 7RD
    Tel: +44 (0)181 442 4133
    Fax: +44 (0)181 442 4155
    Website: www.nlp-community.com